THE RESOURCEFUL TEACHER Series

Christine Frank
Mario Rinvolucri

Creative Writing

Activities to help students produce meaningful texts

HELBLING
LANGUAGES

Creative Writing
By Christine Frank and Mario Rinvolucri
© HELBLING LANGUAGES 2007
www.helblinglanguages.com

ISBN 978-3-902504-99-4

Edited by Jane Arnold
Copy edited by Caroline Petherick
Designed by Gabby Design
Cover by Capolinea

Printed by Bieffe

Every effort has been made to trace the owners of any copyright material in this book. If notified, the publisher will be pleased
to rectify any errors or omissions.

Dedicated to John Morgan, a friend and colleague.

Acknowledgements

I would like to thank the DUET group, who consider creative writing to be a vital part of any English Literature degree course, for a brilliant workshop of theirs that I attended 10 years ago in Norwich.
Thank you also to all the teacher trainees and language students who have written me copious letters over the years for helping me create a "writing climate" in my own head.
Finally I would like to express gratitude to the hugely stimulating teacher group with whom I worked in summer 2006 on the first Pilgrims, Canterbury CREATIVE WRITING course.

Mario

Thanks to Karl Frank for his interest and support and to all the teachers and students in many parts of the world who have tested our material.

Christine

Contents

Contents

Introduction

Menu

Why writing in the classroom?

Over the last fifteen years, the role of writing as an integral part of the learning process has changed radically. Writing used to be seen, in many cases, as a device for testing specific grammar and vocabulary, and so-called 'free writing' was used to assess whether students had successfully made the jump between controlled exercises and uncontrolled text production. Little attention was paid to essential aspects such as why the students wanted to write, in which role they wrote, and the importance of a reader or addressee other than the teacher. The teacher saw his or her role mainly as a provider of feedback concerning the language itself.

Fortunately, however, today we see students in many classes involved in writing for, with or about each other. We as authors believe that this is the right way to proceed, and have been motivated to collect ideas from our classroom experience.

Creating a writing climate

We believe that in tandem with turning your classroom into an island in the school in which it is normal to **speak and listen** in English, it makes sense to also create in your classroom a climate of **communicative writing**.

We write this with a background awareness that some teachers who get their students talking to each other in class in English will content themselves with setting somewhat non-communicative writing exercises; they may, for example, ask students to write a 300-word essay on a theme that they, the teachers, have chosen. They will then take in these compositions and diligently mark them, only to be dissatisfied that the students then pay scant attention to their corrections.

If you want to create a 'writing climate' in your class, modify the above exercise slightly, using this technique from Andrew Wright:

> *Tell each student to weave three lies or pieces of wrong information into their 300 words.*
>
> *When you have (lightly) corrected the compositions, give them back to their authors, and put the students into fours.*
>
> *Student A reads out his or her text, incorporating your corrections. The task of B, C and D is to spot the mis-information. The other three also read their texts, submitting them to their classmates' lie detection.*

The twist of working three lies into the writing humanises this traditional writing exercise. Now, the students will be writing in the knowledge that their classmates will be listening to their content with the beady eye of a detective. Furthermore, these writers now have an audience which may – but does not have to – include the teacher, who can restrict his or her help to matters of form.

A firm principle behind this book is that the writer must always have a reader – and, moreover, a reader who is interested in content, not just form. (In the exercises in Section 5, the addressee is not another person but the writer him- or herself, some time after the time of writing.)

Regardless of the level you teach, there is a lot that you, the teacher, can do to help create a climate of 'writing for real' in your classroom.

Getting to know your students as writers

How do you see *yourself* as a writer? How do you change, as a writer, as you move from mother tongue to the target language? That you are a writer is, of course, beyond doubt; you write or have written some of these:

> *Notes on the kitchen table*
> *Thank you letters/emails*
> *Academic reports*
> *Compositions*
> *Love poems*
> *Stories*
> *Letters you have never sent*
> *Shopping lists*
> *Letters to lawyers*
> *Work emails etc ...*

Since many of us EFL teachers work on writing, it is worth becoming aware of how we see ourselves as practitioners of this skill. On a recent trip to Malaga, south Spain, we, the authors of this book, asked a group of Spanish teachers of English to write short letters explaining how they felt about themselves as writers. We wonder if you will find yourself echoing any of their thoughts, or whether your self-characterisation as a writer would be very, very different.

> Antonio: *I see myself as a hopeless writer. Even sending an email takes me ages, and after sending it, I am never sure I've actually conveyed the message I meant to. Just writing this letter is already a challenging test. I think it must sound as if it were written to an agony aunt asking for help. PS. I have the same problems writing in my own language.*
>
> Macarena: *I'm quite glad you're asking us to write about ourselves, for this early in the morning this seems a much easier task to do. I've always loved writing, I've loved it since I was a child. And I'm not just talking about the typical diary. When I write I seem to be able to free a part of me that does not come out easily otherwise. Writing allows me to admit things that are difficult to express in spoken words. The thing is, it's me I always write to, nobody usually reads me and I don't think I would really like it if they did, either. In fact, the old habit of writing letters to friends is dying out and the quick email is taking over. So much for progress!*

The above texts – which, as mentioned above, were written by teachers – exemplify a fundamental exercise which it is sensible to carry out with any group of students to whom you will be teaching writing skills. It is vital for you, the teacher, to learn something about students' self-image as writers, in both their mother tongue and the target language. To fail to do this is a bit like being an architect who does not much care where he or she is laying the foundations of a house.

It is important that you as a teacher first take a good long look at your own attitude to writing, and then try to find out something about your students' preferences.

Then, when planning lessons, bear both of those aspects in mind.

If you turn to lesson 1, you will find our suggestions on how to get students writing to you about how they see themselves as writers.

Where this book may not be needed

There are some situations in which the way you run a writing class is dictated by events beyond your classroom walls. For example, in Northern Ireland during the recent Protestant/Catholic civil conflict, it was clear that children at primary school, writing in L1, needed to come to terms with the terrifying events happening in their neighbourhood streets. It was these events that they vividly painted in their pictures, and wrote about powerfully and eloquently.

In 1992 we met a training-college teacher of EFL writing from Palestine; he said that his Monday-morning class regularly started with the students writing diary entries about what the Israeli attack planes, bulldozers and patrols had 'achieved' in their West Bank localities over the weekend. These young people had no lack of material to write about.

Zana, in Sarajevo, Bosnia-Herzegovina, wrote this in 1992. She was 12 years old:

> When Daddy is fighting in the War
> If only you knew how it feels
> When your Daddy is fighting in the war
> You run away from unhappiness, but unhappiness follows you
> You hear no news of your father
> And one day when everything is getting black
> Daddy knocks on the door
> Stays for five days
> And then happiness goes away again
> And my heart beats loudly like a little clock
> And now I cannot write anymore because my daddy
> Is not here, close beside me.

(*Letters From Sarajevo*, p 31,
edited by Anna Cataldi, Element Books, 1994
English version of *Sarajevo – Voci Da Un Assedio*,
Baldini e Castoldi, 1993)

In situations of enemy occupation, war, natural disasters, famine, decimation by AIDS and other extreme but all too common situations, what your students are living through may be the driving force in your writing classroom.

The nature of reader-focused writing

Howard Gardner in his seminal book, *Frames of Mind*, suggests that people have both an intrapersonal and an interpersonal intelligence. When an author is alone in his study, working on a book or writing a letter, he is working reflectively in an introspective way; this refers to what Gardner would call intrapersonal intelligence. And yet the author is also aware of the reader's presence. Without *your* presence in our minds, we could not have written this introduction, and this makes the process of writing interpersonal as well.

So, one of the great psychological advantages of addressee-focused writing is that it draws on both the intrapersonal intelligence of students and their interpersonal intelligence.

Most oral work in the target language forces the students, whether they like it or not, into the interpersonal area. In contrast, what could be called the fifth language skill, talking to oneself, draws very largely on the intrapersonal intelligence.

Writing, however, allows the author to **think** and **be** both intrapersonally and interpersonally. It therefore draws on both the introspective and the socially oriented intelligences, as well as, of course, the linguistic intelligence.

Writing in class or writing as homework?

As you flip through the book, you will notice that we suggest doing many of these writing activities in class. In our attempt to humanise the writing part of the curriculum, we feel that, especially for younger people, there should be as short a gap as possible between the act of writing and its being read. When writing is set as homework, there can be a two- or three-day gap between the writing and the reading, and this in many cases greatly detracts from the writing experience – when you cook a soufflé, people need to eat it straight out of the oven!

So we feel it sensible for students to do some writing as homework and some in class time. The advantages for students of working at home are that they choose the moment when they start, they finish when they decide to do so, and they are more likely to be in a reflective state of mind. The advantages of writing in class, on the other hand, are that the students are borne forward by the energy of the group, they are in the presence of their readers, and they can get some of the language help they need from the teacher.

People with a strong intrapersonal intelligence, i.e. the more introspective types, generally prefer home writing, while people with a strong interpersonal intelligence, the more sociable folk, may find writing in class more motivating.

We have met colleagues who feel uneasy about 'wasting good teaching time' by having the students write in class. They feel they are somehow selling the students short. But surely good teaching is taking place when students are fully occupied processing the target language and calling on the teacher when they need him or her? An energised writing activity done in class with the teacher in facilitator role can be a lot more learning-effective than many teacher-dominated phases of a lesson.

We recognise, however, that if you see your class for only 90 minutes a week, as is the case in many Northern European adult classes, you may not want to do much writing in class, and will use the activities in this book for homework. But if you have a group for several hours a week, you might be able to spend more time writing in class. In the case of some students, writing can be a 'springboard' skill which helps them to improve the other four: listening, speaking, talking to self, and reading. This tends to be the case with people who need more thinking time than is allowed by aural/oral interaction.

A model worth proposing to learners of writing
In thinking about our own writing, we have found the Walt Disney model, taken from NLP, to be extremely useful. The great cartoonist was identified by his collaborators as alternating between these states of mind:

> **the dreamer**
> **the realist**
> **the critic.**

If you apply this model to yourself as a writer, how well does it work? Let us lead you into this thinking by means of a few questions:

> *How do you feel as you prepare to write something?*
> *Do you tend to create pictures in your mind prior to writing?*
> *Is dreaming a part of your writing process that you are strongly aware of?*
> *How do you draw up your writing plan?*
> *How do you take the continual decisions that are part of producing text?*
> *Do you like the act of getting something down, making your statements?*
> *As the text in front of you grows, what sort of feelings do you have?*
> *When does the critical voice in your mind chip in?*
> *How useful is this evaluative side of your thinking?*
> *How would your writing be without the critic's contribution?*

This book is partly organised along the lines of the Disney model:

> **Section 1 Getting Going** corresponds to the 'dreamer' stage of the students' process, and offers you many techniques for warming people up into their dreamer phase.
> **Sections 2-6** are about the actual production of the text.
> **Section 7 Editing** is about the students learning to stand away from their text and form a balanced, critical perspective on it.

The Disney model is particularly useful for exam writing, as each student needs to decide how long to allow for the *dreaming,* how long the *realist* text production will be, and how much time needs to be left to the *critic.* A poor dreaming phase will mean thin content, a bad realist stage will mean chaotic writing, and no time left for the critic will result in a text littered with language goofs.

What is in this book?
Section 1 Getting going
Here you will find activities to help you start creating a writing climate in your class, as well as lead-ins to necessary exam skills like composition writing. This section is mainly concerned with preliminary work that facilitates writing in an organised form.
Section 2 Writing from your partner's content
The activities in this section are strongly interpersonal. The student writes from ideas and information proposed by their partner, and they know that their partner will be the main reader of the text.

Section 3 Group writing

There are students who feel the isolation of the writing task to be daunting. The activities in this section are interpersonal and designed to warm such students into feeling good about writing.

Section 4 Writing in role

Those students who enjoy the masks they wear in oral role-play will find writing in role an escape from self, a kind of freeing.

Section 5 Intrapersonal writing

Students who have written diaries in their mother tongue will find these activities easy to get into. This section caters to the student for whom the happiest writing is intrapersonal, the sort of writer who does not need an audience beyond themselves at a later date. This type of writing closely corresponds to interior monologue and dialogue.

Section 6 General writing

In this section you will find techniques for writing practice that take you from the simple drawing up of lists to exploring areas of life experience. The common factor in all these exercises is that the students are exploring their inner world and reacting to stimuli they may not have experienced previously. A highly effective L2 exercise is one in which the students approach a somewhat new area of their own experience, and so are led to develop new thoughts.

Section 7 Editing

This final section is about emerging from the self-involved stage of writing. Achieving distance from one's own text makes it possible to go into critic mode, which focuses students on accuracy and the formal aspects of language.

Using the internet

An excellent way of using the techniques in this book is to link up with a class on the other side of the globe and get the pair-work exercises done with Student A from your class and Student B from the other class. Such work has huge advantages:

(a) your students are using English realistically

(b) your students have the opportunity to make contact with new people

(c) your students are forced out of the cosy cultural assumptions of living in one community, in one corner of one country.

Sharing the ideas in this book with teachers of students' mother tongue

As you look through the acknowledgements that follow many of the activities in the book, you will find that we have learnt much and borrowed much from English mother-tongue creative writing work. Please share ideas from this book with any colleagues you know who teach mother tongue; you may well be helping them to make their classes more interesting.

Enjoy using this book

Finally – enjoy your students enjoying the choreography of the exercises we have presented to you!

SECTION 1
GETTING GOING

Letters in which Students Tell You about Themselves as Writers

Level: Lower intermediate to advanced

Time: 20-30 minutes

Preparation: Write a letter to your students in which you tell them about all the different types of writing you have done in your time: kitchen-table notes, love letters, diary entries, school essays, poems, summaries, text messages, stories you wanted to write, letters of complaint, letters of apology, playscripts etc ...
Tell them how you feel about writing in your mother tongue, and how you feel about writing in English.
Tell them what sort of a writer you reckon you are – keen? reluctant? lyrical? prosaic? creative? careful?
End by asking them to write you a similar sort of letter, one page long, about how they see themselves as writers. Tell them that only you will read this letter.
Copy your letter so each student will get one.

Lesson outline

1. Give the students your letter, and ask them to read it silently. If your written instruction at the end of the letter is clear, they will start writing their replies.

2. Collect the replies, and read them at home with great care. They are full of vital information that will enable you to treat each person in your writing class in ways appropriate to them.
A student who declares that they hate writing in both their mother tongue and English clearly needs more of your support and help than another who says they love the written word in any language.

Rationale
We have found this exercise very useful at the start of a writing class, especially one leading to an important exam.

Preparing to Write about Types of Cleaning

Level: Intermediate and advanced

Time: 20 minutes

Preparation: None.

1. Ask two or three students to come out and, facing the class, to do a one-minute mime of window cleaning, making us imagine the bucket, the cloth, the wiper-blade, and the pane of glass to be cleaned.

2. Call for two or three more volunteers to come out and fully mime brushing their teeth.

3. Put these phrases up on the board:
   weeding the garden
   correcting mistakes in a text
   washing dishes
   disinfecting a wound
   hoovering the carpet.

4. Group the students in fours to brainstorm all the other types of cleaning they can think of; allow 5 minutes.

5. With a 'secretary' from the group at the board, the groups shout out their ideas till the board is covered with cleaning ideas.

6. For homework, ask the students to write the composition: *What I like about my cleaning activities.*

Creative Start to Composition

Level:	Lower intermediate to advanced
Time:	30 minutes
Preparation:	Think of a title for a composition.

Lesson outline

1. Give the whole class the title for the composition.

2. Number your class off: A, B, C, D, E – A, B, C etc.
   Ask the A students each to write seven **questions** about the topic,
   the B students to write seven grammatically **negative** sentences,
   the C students to write seven **declarative** sentences,
   the D students to write seven **exclamations**,
   the E students to write seven **imperative** sentences.
   Allow 10 minutes for the writing phase.

3. Group all the A students, the B students etc. together to listen to each other's sentences.

4. Regroup the students with an A, B, C, D and an E in each group. They listen to each other's sentences.

5. Give the students 10 minutes to write notes towards their composition, drawing on the group's ideas.

6. Set the actual writing of the composition for homework.

Note: This exercise is especially suitable for exam preparation.

Acknowledgement: We learnt the way syntactic forms affect creative thinking from *Sing me the Creation*, Paul Matthews, Hawthorn Press, 1994.

4 A Maelstrom of Letters

Level: Post-beginner to intermediate

Time: 30 minutes

Preparation: None.

1. Ask each student to write their own name on four different slips of paper. Collect the slips and have everybody take someone else's name.

2. Tell them that they are to write a short letter, on any topic – within reason! – that they choose, to the student whose name they have got. As soon as they have finished and signed the letter, they are to deliver it; when a student receives a letter, they should answer it and deliver the answer. Also tell them you will not correct over their shoulders, but that you will help anybody if they ask you. Tell them to begin the writing task immediately.

3. If when a student has delivered their letter they have not got a letter to answer, offer them the slips of paper, to take another name. They write a letter to this person. And so on. You need to work fast and be everywhere in the room!

4. After they have done 20 minutes of sustained writing, tell them that they have 3 minutes left to finish off the text they are working on, and deliver it.

5. Finish with a brief feedback session.

Variation

Bring two classes together in the same space, and ask the students to write only to people in the other group. It is best if they can sit in two long rows, facing each other.

A Sentence from a Picture

Level: Post-beginner to intermediate

Time: 15-25 minutes

Preparation: None.

<table>
<tr><td>Lesson outline</td><td>

1. Ask a 'Picasso' from the group to draw a picture on half of the board. The picture must have some kind of action in it.

2. Students then propose words that come to mind when they look at the picture. A student 'secretary' at the board writes each word on the other half of the board and asks: "Thumbs up or down?" so that the students can show whether they want this word retained. If the majority give 'thumbs down' then the word is erased; if 'thumbs up', it is retained.
This process goes on until there are 10 words on the board.

3. Tell the students to work individually and to write a single sentence using 6 of the 10 words on the board – they may discard 4 words. Tell them that the class will read/hear their sentences.

4. If you have a large class, get the students to stick up their sentences around the classroom walls so everybody can go round and read them. If the group is small, then ask people to read their sentences out.

Variation
Instead of using the words on the board, the students make a sentence using synonyms with, or phrases synonymous to, those on the board.

Acknowledgement: We learnt this technique from Bill Brandt in a workshop in Poland in 1988.

</td></tr>
</table>

A Trip to Remember

Level: Intermediate

Time: 30–40 minutes

Preparation: None.

Lesson outline

1. Put the students into small groups, and ask them to close their eyes and think of a trip they went on as a child.

2. Give the students time to think back, and then ask them the following questions. Tell them not to write the questions down, but to write their answers in note form.
   *What can you remember **seeing** on the trip?*
   *What sounds can you remember **hearing** on the trip?*
   *What **smells** can you remember?*
   *Can you recall how something **felt**?*
   *Can you remember the **taste** of something?*

3. Pair the students, and ask them to relate their experience to their partner, using the notes that they have made; give them 5 minutes to do this.

4. Each student then writes a one-page account of their partner's experience. They write in the first person, as if they were their partner. Tell them these accounts will be read out loud to the group.

5. They read the texts to their group members, and comment on them.

Chapter Headings for my Autobiographies

Level: Elementary to advanced

Time: 30-40 minutes

Preparation: Think of five important areas of your life.
To get you thinking, here are five of Mario's headings:
> *Learning and speaking various languages*
> *Being an elder brother*
> *Reading*
> *Learning ways of managing himself*
> *Being a Dad.*

Then make a list of the five areas of your own life.
Then write a list of 8–12 chapter headings for an autobiography focusing on one of those areas.
Also write a list of 8–12 chapter headings for a general autobiography of your life as a whole.
Copy enough of these two chapter-heading lists so that each student can have their own.

Lesson outline

1. Write up on the board the list of the five areas of your life.

2. Hand out the two lists of your chapter-headings and ask each student to read them.

3. Ask each student to think about their own life, and, as you have done on the board, to write down five roles or life areas that he or she could write an autobiography of. Tell the students they will be sharing these with a small group.
   The student then selects one of their areas and writes 8–12 chapter headings for it. The student also writes 8–12 chapter headings for a general autobiography.

4. Group the students in fours to look at and talk about the two potential autobiographies.

Acknowledgement
We have taken inspiration from the pioneering work of Ira Progoff, *At a Journal Workshop*, Dialogue House, 1975.

8 Concepts

Level: Intermediate to advanced

Time: 45 minutes

Preparation: Think of five concepts – e. g. *peace*, *poverty*, *culture*, *wealth*, *youth* – or choose five concepts from your course book – e. g. *leisure*, *Ireland*, *transport*, *media*, *pollution*.
Write one of each of the chosen concepts on a slip of paper.
Bring in five A3 sheets of paper and enough lined paper for each student to write on.

Lesson outline

1. Divide the students into five groups. Give each group a concept, written on a slip of paper, and a sheet of A3 paper. Tell the students not to show their concept to another group.

2. Ask the students to draw, between them, a picture representing their concept. Make sure every student in the group has the chance to do some drawing. Tell them the drawings will be displayed.

3. As soon as the students have finished, they exchange their picture with another group, but without revealing the concept.

4. Individually, or (if the groups have only 3–4 students) as a group, they describe in writing the drawing they have been given. Tell them that the texts will be displayed.

5. Both the drawings and the texts are put on the wall for all the students to see and read.

6. Invite comments on the pictures and the texts.

7. Get the students to guess what the concepts of the other groups were.

Variation
1. Follow steps 1 and 2 above.

2. Ask the students to brainstorm their concept, noting down 15-20 words on the sheet of paper.

3. Proceed as above, replacing the drawings with the vocabulary that they have suggested.

From My Thoughts to Our Thoughts

Level: Elementary to advanced

Time: 50-60 minutes

Preparation: A sheet of A3 paper for each student, and plenty of coloured pens.

1. Get people up and milling round the room. Ask them to form groups of four or five, but not to choose people they had previously been sitting next to.

2. Give one A3 sheet of paper to each student, and a selection of coloured pens to each group. Ask each person to draw a vertical line down the middle of their page and a horizontal line across the middle, dividing the space into four equal parts.

3. Ask each student to think of a person, an animal, an object, a situation, a book or a film, and then to draw a picture of it in the top left-hand space. Ask them to draw carefully, and to take 5-7 minutes over the drawing. They should then write in a title for their picture. Tell them they will be sharing this with a small group.

4. The students pass their papers to someone else within their group. That person now writes, in the bottom left space, all they **know** about the topic/ person/ object/ book depicted above. They may add to the picture, if they wish. They should write as much as they can in 10 minutes.

5. The students pass the papers round again within their own group, but without taking back their own picture.
First, in the bottom left-hand space, they add anything extra they **know** about the topic/ person/ object/ book.
Then, in the top right-hand space, they write everything they **guess**, **surmise**, or **hypothesise** about it.
They have 10 minutes to do this.

6. They pass the papers around their foursome, without taking a paper they have had before.
They add to the drawing and to the two written spaces.
Then in the last space, they write what they **would like to know** about the person/ topic/ object/ book.
They have 10-15 minutes for this.

7. Ask the fours to get together, read all four papers and discuss the shared information and their own writing processes.

Acknowledgement
We learnt this idea from the head teacher at St Peter's Primary School, Canterbury, in 1999.

10 From Word to Word

Level: Any level, depending on the vocabulary you use

Time: 30 minutes

Preparation: One enlarged copy of the empty frame for each group of students.

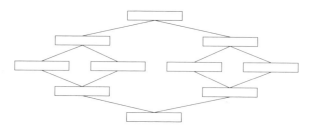

Lesson outline

1. If you are working with vocabulary frames for the first time, you will need to show your students how these work, by doing a couple of examples on the board. You should demonstrate a whole range of possibilities, and so let the students understand that there is no single correct answer.

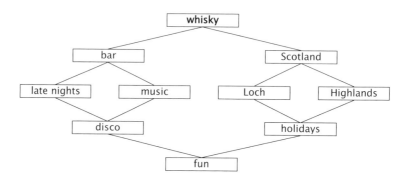

2. Tell the students to think of a keyword, e.g. *freedom*, or any other concept you want to revise. They should then, working individually, list all the word associations that come into their minds; give them 5 minutes to do this.

3. Put the students into groups of two or three, and give each group a copy of an empty frame. They fill in the frame, sharing their ideas.

4. Put two groups together, and let the students in these enlarged groups compare results and comment on them.

5. With a small class, you can have a general discussion, with each group explaining their choice of words.

6. The students individually write a text about the keyword, using all the words in their frame.

First Steps to Essay Writing

Level: Advanced

Time: Two lessons of 45 minutes

Preparation: Cards (as below).

historical	economic	geographical
moral	legal	medical

political

Lesson outline

Lesson One

1. Divide the students into seven groups, so if you have 21 people in your class, there will be three in each group. However, it doesn't matter if the groups are uneven in size – and this lesson plan will work even if it has only one student in each group!

2. Give each of the groups one of the cards.

3. Then write the words from the list below – but write just the first word for now – on the board:
   Drugs
   Unemployment
   Poverty
   Refuse
   Doping in sport
   Homosexuality
   Pollution

4. Let the students think about the word *drugs* in relation to the word on their card.

5. Get the students, in their groups, to write down one or two sentences about this on a slip of paper. Tell them these will be seen by other members of the class.

6. Collect these seven slips, and tell the groups to pass their card to the next group.

7. Write the next word, *unemployment*, on the board, and ask the students to look at it in terms of the new word on their card.

8. Once they have written one or two sentences, collect the slips of paper again and get the students to pass their card on to the next group. Continue with the next word from the list above and so on.

9. While the students are writing, you can be correcting the earlier sentences.

Lesson Two

1. Put the students back into their lesson 1 groups. Give each group the papers relating to a particular topic, e. g. *drugs* for one group, *unemployment* for another, etc. (This means that each of these words will have been commented on from seven different perspectives.)

2. The students read all the information and, as a group, write a coherent text.

Note

With an exam-preparation class, the words on the cards could be changed to match the topics that are likely to come up in the exam.

12 I Live

Level:	Intermediate
Time:	20–30 minutes
Preparation:	None.

Lesson outline

1. On the board, write the following:
   I live …
   I lived …
   I was living …
   I have lived …
   I will be living …
   I would have liked to live …
   I would live …
   I wish I lived …

2. Tell the students to write complete sentences from these beginnings; allow 10–15 minutes for this. Tell them that they will be passing them to their fellow students. While they are writing, go round and make sure they understand what each tense means. If it is a class new to you, you can for your own purposes note down the grammatical forms that need to be revised in future lessons.

3. The students each pass the paper on to their neighbours, who then read these sentences and puts marks by those that arouse their interest and which they would like to know more about.

4. Put the students into pairs to exchange their ideas.

13 Speed Writing

Level:	Elementary to advanced
Time:	10–20 minutes
Preparation:	Think of a topic for the students to write about. Get a stop watch, or a watch with a good second hand.

Lesson outline

1. Be prepared to time a period of 90 seconds. Tell the students they are to write as much as they can in 90 seconds on the topic you are going to give them. They are to write proper sentences, not just lists of ideas. Tell them to try not to lift their pens from the paper. Tell them that nobody else will read what they write.

2. To help students get into the 'speed' mood, get them up and running on the spot for about a minute. Then tell them to sit down, and immediately give them the topic.

3. Stop them after 90 seconds, and ask them to count the number of words they have written.

4. Do a second round, with a new topic and a 120-second time limit.

Rationale
We have used this technique to help people brain-storm before writing an exam composition. Speed writing can help some students get over exam nerves and can also chip away at 'writer's block'.

Acknowledgement
This exercise we learnt from Katie Plumb, a colleague at Pilgrims.

14 Further Steps to Essay Writing

Level: Advanced
The class must have a minimum of 36 students

Time: Two lessons of 45 minutes

Preparation: Lesson 1: if you decide to choose a topic from a course book, you can think up six aspects of it in advance for the students to write about.
Lesson 2: make five photocopies of each of the papers produced in lesson 1, and collate them into sets.

Lesson outline

Lesson One

1. Choose a topic with the students, or use one that may have come up in the course book you are using – e. g: 'emigration'.

2. Divide the topic into six aspects, e.g:
   Disappointment
   Ghettos
   A better life
   Unemployment
   The languages
   The climate.

3. Divide the class into six groups and allocate one aspect to each group; if, for example, if you have 40 students there will be 6-7 in each group.

4. The group members discuss their aspect between themselves, and then as a group write half a page (roughly 100 words) about it. Tell them they will be sharing their writings in small groups.

5. Take in the six half-pages from the groups. Later, you can correct them for language mistakes – but not for content or style.

Lesson Two

1. Re-group the class, ensuring that each student in the new group has written about an aspect of the topic different from every other member of that group.

2. Give a set of the six papers to each group. The papers are passed around the group until each student in that group has read every paper. The students discuss what has been written.

3. Collect all the papers and send the students back to their original seats. They should be given about 20 minutes to write individually on the topic, including as many ideas as they wish stemming from the various aspects.

Variation (a single lesson, for any size of class)

1. Distribute the aspects around the class. This can be done by giving them a number from 1 to 6.

2. The students write half a page individually, and you go round helping and correcting. Tell them they will be sharing their writings in small groups.

3. After about 20 minutes, put the students into groups of six so that all the six aspects are represented.

4. The students read through what the others have written and write a group paper on the topic.

Summary Writing

Level: Intermediate to advanced (for students who have to practise summary writing for an exam)

Time: Lesson 1: 45 minutes
Lesson 2: 45-60 minutes

Preparation: A list of subjects which are of interest to your students, or a list of different topics related to a novel that you have read in class, or a list of exam topics.

Lesson One

1. The students, working individually, choose a subject from the list, and begin writing. The help they need as a class or individually will depend on your writing programme. Tell them that you and another class member will see what they have written.

2. Collect their assignments at the end of the lesson for correction.

Lesson Two

1. Give out the corrected papers, making sure that students do not get their own paper back.

2. Get the students to write a summary of the paper they have received; allow one third of the lesson time for this.

3. As the students finish, swap the initial texts (but not the summaries) so that a second summary can then be written by a different student.

4. The initial text is then returned to its author, along with both summaries. Give the students the opportunity to comment on the summaries of their text, either orally or in writing.

Things People have Written to Me

Level: Elementary to advanced

Time: 30–40 minutes

Preparation: None.

Lesson outline

1. Ask the students to work on their own and write down as long a list as they can under the heading: *Things people have written to me.* Allow them 5–10 minutes. Tell them they will share this with a small group.

2. Ask them to start a new list: *Things I have written.* Again, allow them 5–10 minutes.

3. And then *Things I would like to write,* in another 5–10 minutes.

4. Group them into fours or fives, and ask them to share their lists.

Note
This is a suitable exercise to start a writing course.

Acknowledgement
We learnt the formula from a DUET workshop in Norwich.

SECTION 2
WRITING FROM YOUR PARTNER'S CONTENT

17

A Younger You

Level: Elementary to advanced

Time: 30-40 minutes

Preparation: Prepare cards, each one with an antonym on it, such as:
high low thin thick easy difficult cheap expensive.
Make one card per student.
Copy the instruction text below to give to each student:

First, get up and move around the room looking for a partner who has the word which is the opposite of yours.
You should show your card, but you should not speak.
When you have found your partner, sit down with him/her in silence for 30 seconds.
Then go back to your own seat and write not more than one page about how your partner was when he/she was a young child. (It is up to you to choose the age.)
Exchange sheets with your original partner and respond to what he/she has written. Do not write more than a half page response.
When your partner is ready, move over to him/her and discuss the texts.

Lesson outline

1. Start the lesson silently. Simply give out the cards and the written instructions above.

2. At the end of the paired discussions (see above), allow time for spoken reaction. Adopt a non-directive role.

Rationale
This is a highly interpersonal activity, and students write their pages drawing on a complex mixture of information, deduction, empathy and projection. Best done with a warmed-up class.

18 Drawing a Text

Level:	Intermediate
Time:	45–60 minutes
Preparation:	Copies of two newspaper articles or two anecdotes or two jokes. They should be about the same length, and new to the students.

Lesson outline

1. Divide the students into two groups, A and B. Subdivide A and B into groups of 3–4 students.

2. The students in group A get one text and the students in group B the other. They should not communicate with each other.

3. Get the students to read as a group and discuss the different scenes in the text. They should then draw a picture story showing the scenes in the sequence they occurred. Tell them these will be shared with other groups.

4. Remove the copies of the texts from each group, leaving only the picture stories

5. They should swap the picture story with a group who has worked with the other text and write a **story** from the pictures they have received.

6. At the end you can compare the original stories with the ones they have written.

Note
This procedure is easier if the whole activity – the original text, the picture story and the text from the students – is done on OHP transparencies.

Expanding Sentences

Level: Intermediate

Time: 30–45 minutes

Preparation: None.

1. Get the students to write anonymously about themselves in not more than 5 sentences. If they do not know the other students very well, tell them to write about their lifestyle, their family and their interests. In an established class you can suggest they write about the last weekend, their holidays, etc. Tell them that what they write will be seen by other members of their class.

2. Collect the papers and distribute them, making sure no one gets their own sentences back.

3. They have to read and expand the sentences into a story. It can be as imaginative as the student wants, but they have to include all the information they have from the original student. Encourage the student to write about 200–250 words.

4. Go round offering help and correcting the students' mistakes.

5. They read their stories out. The other students have to listen carefully because the owner has to identify her/himself and explain what is true in the story. If you have over 15 students you can pin up the stories on the wall, and the students can then pick out the story that is about them.

20 From Story to Questions to Story

Level: Lower intermediate to advanced

Time: Lesson 1: 5 minutes
Lesson 2: 5 minutes
Lesson 3: 15– 20 minutes

Preparation: None.

Lesson outline

Lesson One

1. Tell the students, for homework, to bring to mind a story of their own – something that has happened to them or to someone they know. It should be a story that no one else in the class knows.

2. Ask them to write 10 normal comprehension questions about their story – questions that deal with the plot of the story. Tell them to write the questions on a loose-leaf piece of paper. Tell them that these questions will be given to another student.

Lesson Two

1. Pair the students and ask them to quickly exchange sets of questions. They are not to talk about the stories the questions refer to.

2. Tell them, for homework, to write the story they guess/imagine the questions refer to. Tell them to do this without consulting their partner.

Lesson Three

1. Pair the students with the same partner as in lesson 2, and ask them to read each other's stories and to tell the stories that lay behind the questions.

Acknowledgement

We learnt this technique from John Morgan (Obit. Nov 2004).

Ghost-writing

Level: Intermediate to advanced

Time: 30–40 minutes

Preparation: Have envelopes ready, one for each student.

1. Get the students up and moving. Ask them to find a person who they would like to work with for the next half hour. They sit down together and you, the teacher, pair with anybody who is without a partner.

2. Tell each student to prepare to mentally compose a letter to themselves which they will receive in two months' time, on a fixed date. Tell them no one will read the letter they compose except themselves and their partner.

3. They do not write the letter themselves; their partner acts as their scribe and writes it on their behalf. This is not a dictation exercise. Each 'author' gives the partner an outline of what to write, and then both of them write each other's text in a more developed form.

4. When the letters are finished, the authors check them through and correct them, in consultation with their scribe.

5. Give out envelopes for each student to put their letter in. The authors seal the letters and write their names on the outside. You take the letters in and keep them safe.

6. On the date agreed, you bring the letters to class and give them to their authors.

Variation

1. Group the students in pairs as above and then ask the pairs to make fours.

2. The paired students keep together, but move away from the other pair of their foursome.

3. A composes a letter to C, and A's scribe, i.e. B, writes it.

4. B composes a letter to D and B's scribe, A, writes it.

5. C and D do the same, writing letters to A and B.

6. The letters are then given to their addressees, who compose answers that their scribes write.

Rationale

Letters to self are surprisingly powerful, especially with teenagers who are constantly changing. We know of secondary teachers who had students writing letters in September not to be read till the following June.

It is useful for students sometimes to use English in this inner-monologue manner.

The ghost-writing aspect of this exercise provokes the authors of the ideas into a strongly editorial state of mind, in which they really want to make sure the text is as they intended.

Acknowledgement

We learnt this variation from *Letters*, OUP, Burbidge et al., Oxford, 1996.

Hands

Level: Elementary to intermediate

Time: 30–40 minutes

Preparation: Some sheets of paper, A4 or large enough for a hand to spread out on.

1. Get the students into pairs.

2. After you have made sure each student has a sheet of paper ask them to draw around the partner's hands. (If necessary, you could first get a student to draw around your hands on the board.)

3. The students think about what their hands or fingers have done or felt during the past few days. They write notes on their paper 'hands'. Encourage them to use single words or **short** phrases.

4. With their partner, they discuss and elaborate on what they have written.

5. The students then write *A Day in the Life of my Partner's Hands*, including both what has been written and what has been discussed. This task could also be set for homework.

I Take Your Day On

Level:	Post-beginner to intermediate
Time:	30 minutes
Preparation:	None.

Lesson outline

1. Ask each student to write four or five statements about what they did on the previous day. Tell them that these will be shared with a partner.

2. They exchange their papers with a partner, who has to write a paragraph in the first person singular expanding the statements he/she has received.

3. Encourage the students to put themselves in the position of their partner and, by using adjectives and adverbs, write how they felt and reacted in the situations.

4. The papers are returned to their originators, and the students have the opportunity to comment on their reaction to the text.

24 Profiles

Level: Intermediate

Time: 50-60 minutes (this depends on the number of students; with 15 it takes approximately 50 minutes.)

Preparation: A set of questions – each one on a card, one per student – appropriate to the students' age and interests, e.g:
> *Have you ever been involved in a car accident?*
> *What puts you off people?*
> *What toy did you long for, as a child, that you did not get?*
> *If you worked in a zoo, what animal would you like to look after?*

Lesson outline

1. Give each student a different question.

2. Get the students to mill around and ask as many people as possible the question that they have been given. Tell the students to make notes of what each person says. Tell them, too, that the answers will be made available for other people to see.

3. After about 10 minutes, give each one of them the name of a different student in the class.

4. They mill around again, asking for the information about that particular student, e.g:
> *Anna: Steven, did you talk to Linda?*
> *Steven: Yes, I asked her if she had ever been in a car accident*
> *Anna: What did she say?*
> *Steven: She said she had been involved as a passenger last year,*
> *but nobody was hurt. And did you talk to Jens?*
> *Anna: Yes, I asked him what puts him off people, and he said …*

They have about 10–15 minutes to collect as much information as possible about 'their' student. Encourage them to make notes.

5. They then return to their places, so that they can read and order their notes.

6. Next they write a profile of their student. This could be done in class, or set as homework.

7. The next lesson, you can put the profiles up round the room or collect them and produce a class book, which could be circulated to other groups.

Questions to Answer and Questions not to

Level: Elementary to advanced

Time: 30–40 minutes

Preparation: None.

Lesson outline

1. Allow students to get up and mill around the room. Then tell them to get themselves a partner.

2. Ask each student to write a couple of paragraphs about their life that they are happy for their partner to read.

3. Student A (here, female) and student B (here, male) exchange papers. A writes five questions about B's piece, and B writes five about A's.

4. They exchange papers again. A does not answer B's questions, but instead writes a paragraph about each question, commenting on it.

5. A then writes five questions she would have liked B to have asked. Meanwhile B writes comments on A's questions and then the five questions he would have liked A to have asked.

6. The partners exchange papers a third time. They each answer the other's questions (the ones that had been written the first time around).

7. They exchange papers again, read the answers and discuss the whole process.

8. Plenary discussion of the experience.

Acknowledgement
We learnt this activity from Rod Bolitho during a Laurels workshop in Goiania, Brazil.

Reality Changed from Photos

Level: Post-beginner to intermediate

Time: 30 minutes

Preparation: In the lesson before, tell the students to bring in one photo of a member of their family or of a friend.
Take in one or two photos of your own family or friends for any student who has forgotten theirs.

1. Collect the photographs and arrange them on a table.

2. Invite the students to pick up a photo they find interesting, but not their own.

3. They imagine the person in the photo as being one of their relatives or friends. They make rough notes about the person's appearance, age, interests, personality and character.

4. Based on their assumptions and imagination, and using their notes, they write a paragraph about this person and their relationship with him/her. Tell the students this paragraph will be displayed.

5. Put the photographs and the texts on the wall for the students to read and make their comments.

27 Sandwich Story Technique

Level:	Lower to upper intermediate
Time:	40–50 minutes
Preparation:	None, if you use the ready-made story below

Lesson outline

1. Explain to the students that you and they are going to build up a story between you.

2. Dictate this first part:
   The three of them lived together in the village: the mother, the father, and the three-year-old boy. They were not the poorest people in the village. The mother was not a happy woman.

3. Tell the students to write three **grammatically negative** sentences about the family and the village. Tell them that a partner will read what they write.

4. When they've finished, dictate the next bit:
   And then, one day, war was declared and the father had to join the army. What did war mean? What would happen to the man?

5. Tell the students to each write three more **questions**.

6. When they've finished, dictate the next bit:
   The little boy kept asking his mother, "Where has my Daddy gone?" There were many other questions he asked.

7. Tell the students to write two more of the **boy's questions to his mother**.

8. When they've finished, dictate the next bit:
   It was night time and the little boy asked again where his daddy had gone. The mother lit a candle by his bedside, pointed to her own shadow on the wall and said: "Look, there's your Daddy come back."

9. Tell the students to write three **statements** about how the boy and his mother lived.

10. When they've finished, dictate the last bit:
    The soldier was wounded in the war. He came home to the village. He came into his yard and saw his son playing in the dust. He held out his arms to the boy, who said, "Who are you?"
    "I'm your Dad!"
    "No you're not – my Dad only comes at night!"

Sandwich Story Technique

11. Tell the students to write a few sentences to finish the story.

12. Pair the students and ask them to read their stories to each other.

Note
This form of collaborative story-telling allows the students to produce fuller and more correct texts than they could ever do on their own.

Acknowledgement
The first appearance of the sandwich story-telling technique that we are aware of was in John Morgan et al's *Once Upon a Time*, Cambridge, 1985.

28 Things Said or Heard on Holiday

Level: Intermediate to advanced

Time: 40–50 minutes

Preparation: A copy of this questionnaire for each student.

a) I shouldn't have brought so much junk with me. I don't need half this stuff.
b) I wish I'd brought more money.
c) We'll never stay here again!
d) I should have brought some warmer clothes. I didn't know it would be this cold.
e) I should have brought some lighter clothes. I didn't know it would be this hot.
f) I wish we had restaurants like this at home!
g) Do you know how you are supposed to eat this?
h) Don't these people believe in street signs?
i) You can get this for half the price at home.
j) This is such a beautiful place. I'd love to live here.
k) It was nice meeting you. Come and see us when you are in …
l) I never thought a map could be so confusing. I've never been this lost in all my life.
m) They drive like maniacs here!
n) It's a good thing you remembered to bring this along.
o) Remind me to get some postcards tomorrow.
p) This is a real tourist trap. I can't imagine why … told us to come here.
q) I wish all these other people had stayed at home.
r) We didn't come all this way for you to order a hamburger.
s) I'll never go on this type of holiday again.
t) I can't believe it's already time to go home.
u) What's the first thing you're going to do when you get home?
v) We still haven't written any postcards.
w) It's changed a lot since we were last here.
x) Luckily, I didn't need this.

Lesson outline

1. Give the students the questionnaire and ask them to put a tick by any statement they said or heard, exactly or similarly worded, on their last holiday. They may add anything else they said or heard.

2. The students exchange their questionnaire with a partner. Then give them 10 minutes to discuss the situations they ticked.

3. They write an account of their partner's holiday, based on the questionnaire and discussion. Tell them their partner will read this.

4. When the written work is done, they give it back to their partner who has the opportunity to comment on it orally or in writing.

Threesome Stories

Level: Elementary to advanced

Time: 20-40 minutes, depending on the level

Preparation: Supply of A4 paper.

Lesson outline

1. Group the students in threes and give each student an A4 piece of paper on which they should draw a picture that could be the start of a story. Tell them that this, and the stories following, will be passed around the group.

2. Ask the students to pass their picture to their neighbour in the threesome, who should then write a story based on the picture they are given. Make clear that the story needs to be about one page long. There should be no talking at this stage of the exercise.

3. When most people have written about half a page of their story ask them to pass their picture and their half-finished story to another neighbour who then finishes the story.

4. Within the threes they read the three stories thus created.

Acknowledgement
We first experienced this technique with Bonnie Tsai, a Pilgrims colleague, author of *Business Recipes.*

SECTION 3
GROUP WRITING

An Extra Character

Level: Intermediate to advanced (depending on the story)

Time: 45–60 minutes

Preparation: None.

1. Get the students to tell a story that they are all familiar with. It may be a text that has been dealt with in class, a story that is currently in the news, or a traditional story.

2. In groups of three or four, they write the story, putting an extra character into their account. (In one class we were using 'Red Riding Hood', and one group described Red Hiding Hood's twin sister, another group the grandfather and the third group included themselves, who were on a picnic and got involved in the action.) Tell them that these stories will be read by other groups.

3. When they have finished, the members of the groups read each other's stories.

4. Then put one chair at the front and – if the classroom allows it – get the class sitting in a horseshoe around it. This is the 'hot seat'. One person from one of the groups volunteers to play the extra character and to answer questions from the members of the other groups. The volunteer sits in the hot seat and provides answers in role.

31 Everybody Makes a Contribution

Level: Intermediate

Time: 40–45 minutes

Preparation: Supply of A4 paper.

Lesson outline

1. Put the students in groups of six, make sure they've all got paper, and ask each student to write 2–4 sentences about a place, a person or an event important to them. Tell them that these will be displayed.

2. This is passed to the person on the right, who writes about 15 questions.

3. The sentences and questions are passed on again, and the next student answers the questions.

4. The papers are passed on again, and the next student writes a paragraph combining the ideas of the earlier questions with the answers on the topic proposed by the first writer.

5. Once more the papers are passed on, and the next student reads and edits the paragraph, improving the style or the language, e.g. adding adjectives or adverbs.

6. Finally the edited paragraph is passed on to the sixth student in the circle, who draws a picture and who is responsible for the general layout.

7. The six paragraphs plus pictures are exhibited on the walls, so the students have the opportunity to read and learn what has become of their ideas.

Note
If it is impossible to divide your class into groups of six, ask the students to work as pairs.

Expanding Questions and Answers

Level: Intermediate and above

Time: Lesson 1: 25 minutes
Lesson 2: 30 minutes

Preparation: Supply of A4 paper.

Lesson One

1. Give the class a topic that interests them, writing it on the board, e.g.
   My best friend
   Places I have been or
   A teacher who I have known.

2. Let them write, at the top of an A4 sheet of paper, one short
   sentence relating to your topic, e.g.
   My best friend is called Anna.
   Last year I went to Mexico.
   When I was at school, my class teacher was Mr. Evans.
   Tell them that these papers will be passed around and added to.

3. They pass the paper on to the next student, who then writes
   15–20 questions about their statement. Tell them to leave a space
   between each question. At this stage you should go round
   correcting any mistakes they have made. (Don't be tempted to
   reduce the number of questions that they have to write – the last
   ones on their list are often the most interesting.)

4. The papers are passed on again. The recipient reads the
   statement and the questions that go with it, and answers them all
   (inventing answers as he or she wishes). The answers go in the
   spaces left between the questions.

5. As before, you point out any errors that occur, or with a lower-
   level class you might want to take in the papers and correct the
   questions and answers. Make sure the students put their names
   on the papers before they are collected.

Lesson Two

1. Give the papers out, making sure that they don't go to anyone who had them in the previous lesson. The task now is to write an account based on the statement, the questions and the answers received. Tell the students that these will go back to the student who wrote the original statement.

2. The accounts are each given back to the student who wrote the original statement. After having read the account, they can comment either in writing or orally to the whole class.

Rationale

In this activity, the students do not have to concentrate on the content, which frees them to work on style and expression.

Group Holiday Fantasy

Level: Post-beginner to intermediate

Time: 40 minutes

Preparation: A supply of OHP transparencies, one for each 4 students in your class. OHP projector.
Write a short description of a landscape for the students to draw, e. g.

> *In the top left corner of the picture there is a cloud.*
> *The sun is coming out from behind the cloud. You can see about half of the sun.*
> *In the top right-hand corner, draw four birds flying.*
> *Across the middle of the picture there are three mountains in a row from left to right.*
> *On the left side of the right-hand mountain, draw a house.*
> *In the bottom right corner of the picture there is a lake.*
> *On the lake there is a sailing boat.*
> *There is a path leading from the house to the lake.*
> *Halfway along this path there is a gate.*

Lesson outline

1. Dictate the picture to the class, allowing them time to draw what you say.

2. Reconstruct the picture on the board by getting the students to dictate the features to you.

3. Divide the students into two groups, A and B. They make sub-groups of about four students.

4. Tell the students that they all went to this place last year, but half went in winter and half went in summer. (If your climate is tropical, use wet season and dry season.)

5. All the students in group A went in winter/wet and all the students in group B went in summer/dry. Each sub-group of four should write a report from the holiday on an OHP transparency.

6. They present their holidays to the other groups, who should be encouraged to make comments and ask questions.

7. For homework get the students to write a diary entry or a postcard from this communal holiday to someone at home.

Variation
If an OHP is not available, they can write on sheets of paper which you can then put up around the room for the class to read. Tell the students that these sheets are to be displayed.

Group Stories

Level: Elementary to intermediate

Time: 30–40 minutes

Preparation: None.

Lesson outline

1. Get the students to think of words or phrases from a text or topic that has been dealt with recently in class.

2. They should each write down 5 words or phrases from that topic, each word or phrase on an individual slip of paper.

3. Put the students into groups of 5 or 6. The slips are collected, shuffled and put upside down in the middle of the group.

4. Tell each group to decide on a topic of their choice.

5. One student picks up a slip and tells their group a sentence about their topic, using the word or phrase on the slip.

6. The students continue one after the other, trying to make a coherent text, until most or all of the slips have been used up.

7. Based on this oral production, each group writes a text to be read by the other groups.

8. Allow time for class comment or discussion.

Words to Text

Level:	Post-beginner to intermediate
Time:	30-40 minutes
Preparation:	None.

Lesson outline

1. Give the students a topic, e.g. *a film*, *the last lesson*, *the latest news*, etc.

2. The students are to build a sentence. This is done by each student in turn saying one word, e.g:
   A *Last*
   B *Last week*
   C *Last week I*
   D *Last week I went, etc.*

3. Intervene if there are any mistakes or if the sentence gets too long. Do not let students write during this phase.

4. When the sentence is finished, ask them to write it down.

5. Go on to the next sentence in the same way, i.e. the students take it in turns to add a word to build the sentence, and then they all write it down.

6. After about four to five sentences, tell the students to work individually and to combine what they have written into a short story or text. They can write one or two additional sentences at the beginning, in the middle or at the end, but they must not alter the original sentences.

Writing a News Story

Level: Intermediate

Time: 45–60 minutes

Preparation: Over a week, tear out pictures from newspapers, showing local, national or international news. Stick each picture onto an A4 sheet of paper. With a small class (under 15 students) offer one picture per student. With more than 15 students have one picture per pair.

Lesson outline

1. Give out the pictures. If you have more pictures than students in the class, let them choose which they want.

2. Tell them to look at their own picture and write down four or five words or phrases that spring to mind. They write their ideas on the sheet beneath the picture. Tell them that these will be passed around the class.

3. They pass the paper on to their neighbour, who reads the words/phrases and adds four or five of her/his own. Then the picture is passed on again and other items are added. This procedure is repeated about eight times, until there are about 30–40 phrases altogether. It becomes increasingly difficult for the students to come up with additional ideas, but usually their contributions will be more interesting towards the end.

4. Each picture is given back to the original student, who then has a resource with which to write a short text arising from the words and/or the picture. The writing can be done in class or as a homework activity.

Variation (for advanced classes)
While the pictures are going round, the students should decide whether their words are fact or opinion, and list them accordingly in one of two columns on the sheet. This may influence the writing process.

SECTION 4
WRITING IN ROLE

'Days of the Week' write to 'Months of the Year'

Level: Elementary to intermediate

Time: 30–40 minutes

Preparation: None.

Lesson outline

1. Ask a student to put the months and the days of the week, out of order, up on the board.

2. Designate half the class as months: "Shiho, you are March; Marek, you are February," etc. (It doesn't matter whether there are too few students or too many – you can leave out some months or use some twice.)
   With the other half of the class, allocate them days of the week. Ask each student to get a partner in the other half of the class, but then to go back and sit in their normal place.

3. Each student, in role as e.g. December or Wednesday, writes a one-page letter to his or her partner, asking this person what it is like to be that particular day or month, e.g. Wednesday or December, and telling them how their own time period is better.

4. When they have finished their letters, they exchange texts and write replies.

5. The partners come together, read the replies and discuss the experience.

Variations
Students with an interest in language could choose which punctuation mark to be e.g. ( ) ; , : ! ? . " " – / etc. They write letters to other class members in role as the punctuation they have chosen, and bearing in mind the punctuation role of their addressee.
With a group of chemists we used the Periodic Table in a similar fashion. One student took on the role of **au** (gold) while another became **pb** (lead).
With musically inclined people, you could ask them to become instruments of their choice, or notes: for example, one student could be a minim, another a semi-quaver.

A Disguised Hand

Level: Post-beginner to intermediate

Time: 30–40 minutes

Preparation: None.

Lesson outline

1. Get two or three students to walk around at the front of the class, without telling them why. Ask the others to comment on the ways they walk.
   Point out to the students that ways of walking are characteristic to the walker, just as ways of reading are.
   Get two or three students to read a short paragraph from the textbook. Ask the others to comment on voice use.

2. Ask each student to copy out one paragraph from the course book and sign it. Tell them these will be displayed.

3. The paragraphs are stuck up on the walls, and everybody goes round having a really good look at their classmates' handwriting.

4. Each person writes a three-paragraph letter to someone of their choice in the class. Tell them that the letter will be seen by others, as well as by the addressee. They do not sign it, and they write it in disguised handwriting. One way of doing this is to deliberately imitate the handwriting of a parent, boy or girl friend, or sibling.

5. The letters are put in a pile and each person takes one letter, but not their own. Their task is to guess who the writer was. To do this they go round and compare the handwriting with the samples displayed on the walls. Then they check with the person they think it belongs to.

6. Finally, the letters are given to their addressees.

Rationale
The way you walk, the way you eat, the way you use your voice and your handwriting are all aspects of who you are. For some readers, handwriting can be a significant part of a written message – a part that is lost in using a keyboard.

Acknowledgement
Simon Marshall set us on the road to thinking up handwriting exercises.

From Group Picture to Dialogue Writing

Level: Post beginner to elementary

Time: 30–40 minutes

Preparation: None.

Lesson outline

1. Tell the students that as a group they are going to produce a picture on the board. Each person can draw one element in the picture, e.g. a person can draw a tree, but not a ladder leaning on it as well. Students come out one after the other. Those who drew something early in the process can have another turn later.
   Your role is to stand back, enjoy your own silence and observe.
   End the process when 15–20 elements have been drawn.

2. Ask for a 'secretary' to come out, and, with the help of the group, name each object/ animal/natural feature and write the name in. Here again, you can take a back-seat role.

3. Pair the students.
   Ask them to think individually of some feature, animal, or object in the picture that they associate with.
   Each student assumes that role, and writes the first line of a dialogue that might take place between it and the role chosen by his or her partner. (So, for example, the sun might write to a pond.) Tell them that they might act out their dialogue in front of the class.

4. After writing the first line of their dialogues, the paired students swap papers.
   They write a response, still in role.

5. Ask them to keep swapping until they have filled a page with each dialogue.

6. Get three or four pairs round the group to act out their two dialogues, each taking their own part.

Variation 1
Ask students, working individually, to make up a dialogue between two features of their choice from the picture. The individual student writes both sides of the dialogue.

Variation 2

Ask students to think of the picture as frame 3 of a picture story. They draw frames 1, 2 and 4, and then write the story.

Variation 3

With higher-level students, ask them to a write a private diary of how they felt as they watched the group picture take shape. In the build-up of the picture, there can often be a complex interplay of aggressive and cooperative behaviour.

Gazing in the Mirror

Level: Intermediate to advanced

Time: Lesson 1: 2 minutes
Lesson 2: 40–50 minutes

Preparation: None.

<h2>Lesson outline</h2>

Lesson One

1. Ask the students to find a mirror at home, take a good long look at themselves and then write a very objective, scientific description of their own face. Tell them that this will be seen by other class members.

2. Tell them to bring this, along with a hand mirror, to the next class.

Lesson Two

1. Ask the students to pair up with a classmate they get on with, and sit facing each other. Each student writes a half-page description of the other's face. Tell them that this, and the further texts they are to write, will also be seen by other class members. Make it clear that you are available to help with language, but that you will only come over when invited to.

2. Ask them, working alone now, to look in their hand mirror, and write a really flattering self-portrait. It should be about half a page, and written from the point of view of someone who really likes them.

3. Ask each student now to imagine they belong to another race or are an extra-terrestrial, and to write three very negative descriptive sentences about their own face.

4. Bring the pairs together into fours to compare the four texts each has written.

Note

You will find a similar exercise, using a video camera rather than mirror, in *Video*, Cooper et al., Oxford, 1989.

Same Event – Different Points of View

Level:	Intermediate to advanced
Time:	30–45 minutes
Preparation:	None.

Lesson outline

1. Dictate this text to your class:
   John had just passed his driving test. It was a wet day and John had been driving for three hours. He came to this bend in the road; the car went into a skid, turned turtle and burst into flames. Luckily, John was catapulted out of the driving seat and landed in a bush.

2. Write these 8 roles up on the board:
   John's driving instructor
   Local road engineer
   John's granny
   Tyre-company researcher
   John
   John's therapist
   Car-production engineer
   John's girl friend

3. Explain to the students that different people will tend to attribute different causes to the same event. Ask each student to choose two of the roles from the board and write half a page about why the accident happened. They write in the first person, as the granny or the car production engineer etc. Tell them that these texts will be read by other class members. Give them a time limit of 15–20 minutes.

4. Ask the students to work in fours, reading out to their group their eight texts.

5. Round the lesson off by asking three or four people who have all chosen the same role to read out their texts to the entire class.

Acknowledgement
This exercise was inspired by an idea in *Why do Men Barbecue? Recipes for Cultural Psychology*, Richard Shweder, Harvard University Press, 2003.

Second-Guessing the Answer

Level: Lower intermediate to advanced

Time: 30-40 minutes

Preparation: String cut into 30-cm lengths, one per pair of students.

1. Randomly pair your students; hold up the strings by their mid-points and ask each student to grab an end but not to pull. Let go of the strings, and the students are randomly paired.

2. Ask the paired students to sit across the room from each other.

3. Ask each student to write a one-page letter to his or her partner.

4. Ask the pairs to exchange letters, and ask each person to write a four-sentence reply to the letter just received.

5. Then ask each student to write the four-sentence answer he or she **expects** their partner to have just written.

6. The partners get together and read all six letters.

7. If there is time, allow a brief feedback session on the activity.

The Whole Writes to the Parts

Level: Intermediate to advanced

Time: 30–45 minutes

Preparation: None.

Lesson outline

1. Divide the students up into groups of three. Ask them to decide who is A, who is B and who is C.
   Tell the students to move away and sit some distance from their partners.

2. Tell them that all the As are the **car,** all the Bs are the **steering wheel**, and all the Cs are the **brakes**.
   The car is to write a half-page letter to the steering wheel and another to the brakes.
   The steering wheel is to write half-page letters to the car and the brakes.
   The brakes write half-page letters to the car and the steering wheel.
   Tell them that these letters will be shared around their group.

3. Tell the students to deliver their letters to their partners as they finish writing.
   Each student will then have two letters to reply to.

4. At the end of this second writing phase, get each threesome back together to read the responses and to comment on the whole activity.

Variation

Instead of the students working in threes, have them work in pairs, and ask the **whole** to write to one **part**, and vice-versa. They write one-page letters. So you could have correspondences between:

- Volcano & Lava
- River & Source
- Drunkard & Liver
- House & Roof

Acknowledgement
We learnt the variation from *Letters*, Burbidge et al. OUP, 1996.

Victim–Persecutor–Rescuer Dialogues

Level: Lower intermediate and above

Time: 20–30 minutes

Preparation: Check you have the translations for *Victim*, *Persecutor* and *Rescuer* in the students' mother tongue.
Copy each of these dialogues onto separate slips of paper, enough for one slip per threesome.

> *I'll be here for you.*
> *I'm leaving you.*
> *I think I'm pregnant.*
>
> *You have simply got to pay me.*
> *I can't pay.*
> *Listen, I'll help you; I'll pay.*
>
> *I never have enough money.*
> *You've spent your pocket money! Not a penny more!*
> *I can lend you a fiver.*

Lesson outline

1. Group the students into threes and give out the slips, so each threesome has one dialogue. Tell them they will be acting these out in front of the rest of the class, and give them 7 minutes to decide the following:
    who is speaking each line
    their relationship with the other two
    the time of day
    where they are
    how to say their lines.

2. Several threesomes come to the front and act out their lines. Ask each threesome to act the little scene twice. Give out the rest of the slips, so each group of three has all three scenes.

3. Write *Persecutor Victim Rescuer* on the board, and add the mother-tongue translations.
Ask the students to identify who is the persecutor in each conversation, who the victim, etc.

Victim–Persecutor–Rescuer Dialogues

4. Tell the threesomes to come up with three more three-line persecutor/victim/rescuer conversations, and to prepare to act them out convincingly.
Go round and help with language.

5. Performance time!

Acknowledgement
We are grateful to Jim Wingate for teaching us this set of ideas from Transactional Analysis.

Views of a House

Level: Elementary to advanced

Time: 30–40 minutes

Preparation: Be ready to tell the students a description of your own home, as seen by someone who really likes it, and a second description of your house, as seen by some one who does not like it.

Lesson outline

1. Give the students the first description of your own home.

2. Ask them to bring to mind a person who really likes their house or flat. Ask them to write three paragraphs to a page about their house, in the words of that person. Tell them they will be sharing these in groups.

3. Give the students the negative description of your home.

4. Ask them to write a description of their place seen through the eyes of a person who they think does not like their house or flat; again, these will be shared.

5. Group the students in fours to listen to what their classmates have written.

Variation
The writing is done not about your house but about you yourself, first from the point of view of someone who likes you, and then from the point of view of someone who does not.

Acknowledgement
We learnt the variation above from the UK radio programme, *Thought for the Day*.

Writing to a Role

Level: Lower intermediate to advanced

Time: 20–40 minutes

Preparation: None.

Lesson outline

1. Ask for a volunteer to think about what they would most want to be, right now, if they could suddenly become an object, an animal or a different person, and tell this to the class.

2. Once she or he has done this, ask each of the other students to write one question addressed to the volunteer in role. If she or he has decided to become a seagull, then students might write things like:
   How much time do you spend on the water?
   Do you have one mate or many?

3. The students put their questions to the volunteer, who answers in role.

4. Ask each student to write a half-page letter to the volunteer, who, while they are doing this, writes an example of the sort of letter he or she expects to receive from them. Tell them these letters will be read out to the class.

5. Ask between 5 and 10 students to read out their letters. The volunteer then reads the letter he or she wrote.

6. If there is time, allow a general feedback discussion.

Acknowledgement
This exercise is a development of one in Section 3 of *Letters*, Burbidge et al., Oxford, 1996.

Writing to Grammar Words

Level: Elementary to advanced

Time: 30–40 minutes

Preparation: None.

1. Brainstorm grammar words and put them on the board, e.g:

   adjective   *conjunction*   *present simple*
   comparative   *article*   *adverb*
   verb   *noun*   *past participle*

2. Randomly pair your students and ask them to work individually, and decide which grammar word best suits the personality of that classmate. Suppose that Student X decides that Person Y is a typical conjunction, they then start a letter to him/her like this:
   Dear Conjunction, ..."
   The content of the letters the students write is up to them.

3. As soon as a letter has been written it is delivered.
   On receiving a letter, the recipient replies.

4. Encourage the students to write to as many other bits of grammar as they can in the time available.

Variation

Brainstorm any set of items, e.g:

- vegetables: (*Dear Cauliflower,*)
- parts of an aircraft (*Dear Aileron*)
- military ranks (*Dear Lieutenant*)
- furniture (*Dear Sofa*)
- months of the year (*Dear April*)
- flowers (*Dear Daffodil*)

Written Two-way Dialogue

Level: Elementary to advanced

Time: 30-40 minutes

Preparation: Supply of A4 paper.

1. If possible, seat the students in a circle. If you have fixed benches, the exercise can still be done with the students in their rows.

2. Describe a situation in which a parent is waiting up for an early-teens child to come back home at night. The clock strikes midnight and no child appears. The parent brews coffee and get more and more worried. Two o'clock passes. Still no teenager. Finally, at 3.05 am, the door opens and in walks the teenager. Ask the students to think of what they would say at this moment, as the parent.

3. Check each student has an A4 sheet of paper, and ask them to write down at the top of it the parental reaction they think is most likely. Tell them these will be passed around, and may be read out. Ask each student to pass the paper to the person on their left (or behind, if sitting at the end of a row). The person receiving the paper is then to write the teenager's response to the parent.

4. Everybody in the room has now written the teenager's line of dialogue.
   Everybody now passes their bit of paper back to the person on their right. This person, who is the one who wrote the first parental sentence, now writes their response to the teenager. The activity continues with each student involved in two separate written dialogues, one with their 'child' and one with their 'parent'. (Each student has their 'child' on their left and their 'parent' on their right.

5. Stop the activity when about one to one and a half pages have been filled, and before the writers start flagging. Ask a few volunteers to read their dialogues to the class. Each person reads their own part.

Written Two-way Dialogue

Variation

You can use this technique over and over again with other binary-conflict situations, e.g.

- Speeding motorist v policewoman
- Teacher v student who rarely does homework
- Wife v husband
- Brother v sister
- Evasive politician v probing journalist.

Acknowledgement

We first published this exercise in *Grammar in Action Again* back in the 80s. We learnt the technique from *Towards Self-understanding*, Malamud and MacHover, Charles C. Thomas, Illinois, 1965.

Your Picture, My Story

Level: Elementary to advanced

Time: 30–40 minutes

Preparation: None.

Lesson outline

1. Ask the students, working individually, to recall an incident from the past. Next, they spend five minutes drawing the incident, either in a single picture or as a strip cartoon.

2. Students get up and move around the room. They find a partner, exchange drawings without discussing them, and then go back to their previous places.

3. Ask each student to write a page telling the story of the incident in their partner's drawing. They write the account in the 'I' form, as the other person. Tell them these will be shared.

4. The partners read each other's accounts and then tell their own stories.

Acknowledgement
The idea in Step 1 is one we learnt from Tom Mohan, writing in the Beitraege section of the last *Zielsprache Englisch* in 1999.

SECTION 5
INTRAPERSONAL WRITING

Happy Chair, Sad Chair

Level: Elementary to advanced

Time: 20–40 minutes

Preparation: None.

1. Ask your students to relax and take up a comfortable sitting position.
   Tell them to shut their eyes and visualise a chair – any chair. Now ask them to imagine the chair in a scene from a comic film or an amusing story.
   This picture fades. Ask them to imagine a chair in a neutral scene, neither happy nor sad.
   Ask them to see a chair in sad, tragic scene.

2. Ask them to switch from the sad scene back to the comic one. Ask them to do this mental switching several times. End with the cheerful scene.

3. They now write a page about how the experience was for them. Tell them they may choose whether their writing is kept private or read out to the class.

4. Those who want to read to others what they have written now do so.

Rationale
The exercise invites students to notice how they visualize and emotionally contextualize a scene. Not everybody is conscious of this. Exercises that have students doing something that they haven't done before in their mother tongue are particularly effective in second-language learning.

An Experience that Leads to Intrapersonal Writing

Level: Intermediate to advanced

Time: 30-40 minutes

Preparation: For Variation 2, bring in three short snatches of music (2-3 minutes each), and the equipment to play it.

Lesson outline

1. Get the students up onto their feet. Ask for a volunteer, and stand behind them. Ask them to move their right hand, and follow the movements with your own right hand. Explain to the group that you are trying to follow your partner as closely as possible, so sometimes you anticipate their next movement.

2. Pair the students, and ask them to do the mirroring exercise for 45 seconds. Then ask the leader to become the follower for another 45 seconds. Ask for silence during the exercise.

3. To get the students reflecting, say:
   I wonder how you felt during the mirroring.
   I wonder if you preferred leading or following, and why.
   I wonder how it felt to be in harmony with another person.
   I wonder if either of you felt aggressive.

4. Ask them to sit down and, using their answer as a springboard, write a two-paragraph diary entry that only they will see.

5. After five minutes' writing time, ask for another volunteer and demonstrate two-handed mirroring, facing your partner. When mirroring is done well, there is no clear leader or follower. Ask them to find new partner and do this exercise for two minutes with them; time it.

6. To get the students reflecting, say:
   Did we divide the space between us equally?
   Did one of us become the leader?
   How did I feel?
   And the other person?

7. Then they write a two-paragraph diary entry, starting with their answers.

8. Ask them to repeat the face-to-face mirroring exercise with a new partner.

9. Ask them to write a third diary entry, but this time summing up how the whole experience has been for them.

10. Round off with an open discussion.

An Experience that Leads to Intrapersonal Writing

Variation 1

1. Pair the students and ask them to go for a 10-minute 'blind walk' round the school; one student in each pair is blindfolded and their partner guides them, making sure they are safe. After 10 minutes, they swap roles.

2. They come back into the classroom and write a one-page diary entry. Again, strictly private, so they can really be as open and sincere as they want.

3. End with a brief discussion, as by now some will be bursting to speak and share their thoughts.

Variation 2

1. Play the first piece of music twice, and then ask the students to write half a page about their reaction to it; again, strictly private.

2. Play the second piece once: they write their reaction.

3. Play the third piece twice: they write their reaction to all three pieces together.

Variation 3

1. 15 minutes before the end of a lesson, write this outline up on the board:
   The rhythm of the lesson
   Moments when I felt interested
   Moments when I felt bored
   Moments of good feeling with other people
   Moments of bad feeling with other people
   Anything unexpected that happened
   What sort of animal/fish/bird was I like this lesson?
   What sort of weather was the teacher like?

2. Ask them to write a 10-minute diary entry about any of the above aspects of the lesson that interest them, or any other aspects of it.

An Experience that Leads to Intrapersonal Writing

Rationale

We can hear some colleagues asking, "What's the point of students doing secret writing that remains uncorrected?"

We feel that to introduce the foreign language into the student's communication with him- or herself is a major step in her beginning to 'be' in English, rather than just manipulating components of language. When people write to themselves in a foreign language, the very act of doing this makes the foreign code feel less foreign. Maybe you remember the first time you realised you were talking to yourself in a foreign language you were learning. We also feel it is very important that some student writing should be beyond the reach of the teacher's red pen, that they should not be writing 'for correction' but purely for self-expression.

Note

If you ask your students to do 'diary entries' from time to time, it makes sense to give them occasionally a 10-minute oasis in class to go back and re-read what they have written – just re-read it, silently.

Do I Like Doing This?

Level: Elementary to advanced

Time: Lesson 1: 5 minutes
Lesson 2: 15 minutes

Preparation: Try the exercise out yourself before asking a class to do it.

Lesson One

1. For homework, ask students to be aware, between this lesson and the next, of their state of mind each time they turn an electric switch on or off. Explain that they should ask themselves the question:

    Do I like what I am doing/ feeling/ thinking at this moment?
    For example, a parent, entering a kitchen first thing in the morning and turning the light on to find dirty dishes left by a teenage son who has decided to cook himself a midnight feast, may, if the room had been left clean and tidy the night before, feel disgust, rage or frustration!
    The question could be asked of any routine task that is performed several times a day. It does not have to be about switching on a light.

Lesson Two

1. Ask the students to work on their own and write down some of what they remember thinking or feeling at those moments. Tell them that their writing will be entirely private. No one will see what they have written. Tell them you are available if they need language help, but you will not look over their shoulders at what they are writing. Allow 10–20 minutes for this task.

2. When they finish writing, have a general feedback session about how the self–observation and the writing went.

Note

Writing things in English that will only be read by the student him- or herself is a very important step in making the language their own, in appropriating it, and this is in turn something that creates enjoyment and accelerates the learning progress.

Improving on Reality

Level: Elementary to advanced

Time: Lesson 1: 20–30 minutes
Lesson 2 (*a month later*): 5–10 minutes

Preparation: Think of a situation you are ready to share with your students, a situation where things did not go as you wanted them to go.
Prepare to tell them about this situation.
Also prepare to tell them how you would have liked the situation to have gone.
Bring envelopes to class, one for each student.

Lesson outline

Lesson One

1. Tell the students about a personal situation in which you were not satisfied with the way things went. Now replay the situation to the class as you would have liked it to have gone. Explain that we often do something of the sort in our heads.

2. Ask the students to bring to mind a negative situation and to replay it to themselves as they would have liked it to have gone. Ask each of them to write a page about the improved situation as they've imagined it. Tell them that no one but them is ever to see this piece of writing.

3. When they finish writing, give them each an envelope and explain that they will get their texts back in a month's time. They seal their text in their envelope and put their names on the front. You collect the texts and keep them safe.

Lesson Two

1. Give back the envelopes.

2. Allow the students to give you any feedback they want about the impact of reading what they wrote a month back.

Letters to Self

Level: Intermediate and above

Time: Lesson 1: 20 minutes
Lesson 2: (*in the final lesson of the course*) 15 minutes

Preparation: Think of some questions for your students to consider, eg:
Which fellow students do I empathize with?
Which students would I find it harder to work with??
Which students do I find attractive or interesting?
Which student is most like me?
How much would I reveal about myself in class?
Does the teacher behave like a teacher I have had before?
Does the teacher talk a lot?
Are my goals in the class realistic?
How much do I want to invest – time, energy, myself?
Where do I want to be at the end of the course?
The questions above are only a rough guide, and you should choose your questions carefully, depending on the class.

Lesson outline

Lesson One
1. Get the students to relax and sit quietly. If it seems appropriate in your teaching situation, tell them to shut their eyes.

2. Tell them your questions.

3. Leave the students a few minutes to think about these questions.

4. Tell them to write a letter to themselves about what they can expect from the course. Be sure to stress that the letters are private, and that no one else is to read them. Allow 15 minutes.

5. Give out the envelopes and get them to write their names on them.

6. Collect these letters and keep them for the final lesson of the course.

Lesson Two
1. Distribute the letters again, and allow the students time to read them.

2. If they want to comment on the content, it can be the basis of feedback.

Note
Lesson 1 is best done only after the students have had the chance to introduce themselves and get to know each other and their teacher.

SECTION 6
GENERAL WRITING

A Composition with No Verbs

Level: Lower intermediate to advanced

Time: 30-45 minutes

Preparation: Be ready to describe a house you have lived in, but without using verbs.
It might go like this:
High ceilings, typical of late 19th century.
Very quiet. Noise in one place, quiet everywhere else.
Lots of space, and cool in summer ...

1. Ask the students to listen carefully to what you are going to say next, and tell you which grammatical category you are not using. Then describe the house of your choice **verblessly**.

2. Check that the students have noticed the omission. Then ask each of them to write a half-page description of a house they know well, leaving out verbs. Tell them these will be shared in groups.

3. Group the students in fours or fives to listen to each other's texts.

Rationale
This is a syntactic awareness exercise: you notice the role that a part of speech actually plays when you are required to avoid it. Working largely in noun phrases alters the way you think and create, and illustrates the fact that arbitrary limitation can actually foster creativity.

Acknowledgement
We learnt this exercise from *Sing me the Creation*, Paul Matthews, Hawthorn Press, 1994.

A Flower Family

Level: Lower intermediate to advanced

Time: 40–50 minutes

Preparation: Take 3 or 4 vases into class, with around 20 of one type of flower but with, if possible, some colour variation between the individual flowers. (For example, red and white varieties of roses would be better than daffodils.)
If your teaching situation does not allow you to bring flowers into the classroom, collect about 20 pebbles instead.

Lesson outline

1. Place the flowers and vases where everybody can see them. Ask a volunteer flower arranger to come and put the flowers into the vases.

2. Group the students in threes and tell them that the flowers represent an extended family. For example, two of the flowers could be the parents etc. Ask them to spend 5 minutes discussing the idea each of them has of the family.

3. Ask the students, working individually, to write a page about the family, a part of the family or about one or two family members. Give them 20 minutes for this. Tell them these will be shared in groups.

4. Ask the people in the threesomes to read their pages to one another.

5. In plenary, ask the students to discuss their impressions of the flower family/ies.

Note
We have tested this exercise with well-warmed up groups and have found it brings out quite strong emotion, so it would not be sensible to do it with an unwarmed-up class.

Dialogue into Dialogue

Level: Intermediate

Time: 30–40 minutes

Preparation: Take in a dialogue suitable for the class. This may be from the course book, or it may be one that a student has previously written.

1. Divide the class into two groups, A and B.

2. Invite two students to the front, and give them, taking the roles of speakers A and B, a dialogue to read out to the class.

3. The dialogue is read at normal speed by the chosen students. Group A writes down what student A says in the dialogue, and group B notes what student B says. The students work individually and get as much down as possible.
   With a low-level class, it may be necessary to have the dialogue read twice.

4. The students have a moment to compare and complete their half of the dialogue with the others in their group.

5. Working individually and using the half of the dialogue they have, the students then make up the other half. So the members of group A write the part of speaker B and the B-group that of speaker A. This can be done in any way they like, and **does not have to resemble the original**. This should be done on a new sheet of paper. Tell them that these will be performed in front of the class.

6. Put the students into pairs (one each from group A and group B), allowing them only to take the paper with the freely written text with them. They then create a new dialogue, using what they have written. After making any necessary changes to the new dialogue, they perform it for the class.

Different Ways of Thinking about the Same Object

Level: Elementary to advanced

Time: 30–40 minutes

Preparation: Take half a dozen objects to class; e.g: a handbag, teapot, stone, small branch etc.

Lesson outline

1. Put the objects on a surface, and write these instructions on the board:
   Choose one of the objects, and write, about that object:
   - *three **sad** sentences*
   - *three **false** sentences*
   - *three **clear**, **objective** sentences*
   - *three **very simple** sentences, as if you were five years old*
   - *three sentences **as if you were in your 90s**.*
   Write three of these groups of sentences in your mother tongue.
   Write the other two groups of sentences in English.
   Tell them that they will be sharing their sentences with the class.

2. Allow adequate time for the writing, and when the students have finished, put them into pairs, and ask them to swap papers and then translate their classmate's MT sentences into English. Encourage the pair to collaborate. Be available to help with language.

3. Re-group the students according to the objects they have written about, and ask them to pass round the English versions of their texts.

Note
If you have a multi-mother-tongue class, you may have some mother-tongue isolates (i.e. nobody else speaks their MT). In their case, in step 2 above, they will translate their own MT sentences into English.

Acknowledgement
We thank the Steiner tradition and Martin Matthews in *Sing me the Creation*, Hawthorn Press, 1994, for this activity.

Falling

Level:	Lower intermediate to advanced
Time:	40–50 minutes
Preparation:	Write a page about a fall you remember and copy this to give to the class.

1. Ask the students to use the board and brainstorm all the falls they have had. Here are some you might add to theirs:
   falling out of a pushchair
   falling out of a boat
   falling down the stairs
   falling off a swing
   falling off a wall
   falling off a high diving board
   falling off a camel.

2. Give them your text to read.

3. Ask them to work individually and list the falls they have had in their lives. Each student is to then pick one of those situations and write a page about it; tell them this will be displayed to the class.

4. Ask the students to stick what they have written up round the walls and immediately return to their seats.

5. Group the students in threes and ask them to tell each other about exactly how and why they chose to describe the fall they did.
   Now ask each student to tell their partners the story of the chosen fall, but this time focusing on it differently.
   Leave the students' imaginations free by resisting the temptation to define what you mean by 'differently'.

6. Now they go and read the original texts on the walls.

Rationale
If some students compose a text about the same reality from two different angles and other students produce a text with a more detailed and more complex view of reality, this offers itself for discussion in class.

From Emotion to Situation

Level: Elementary to advanced

Time: 40–50 minutes

Preparation: None.

Lesson outline

1. Ask the students to work on their own and to make a list of emotions, e.g:
   joy
   jealousy
   fear
   surprise
   anger
   reverence

2. Working in fours, they compare and enrich their lists.

3. Tell them to work on their own now, and cross off the list any emotions they have infrequently experienced.

4. Pair the students, and ask them to tell each other of times when they have experienced one or two of the emotions left on their lists.

5. Ask them to tell each other what sensory channels they associate with each emotion. Do they see mental pictures, feel things or internally hear things?

6. Tell them to work individually and to write a page about one occasion when they experienced one of these emotions vividly. Tell them these will be shared with their group.

7. Ask the students to make the same foursomes as before and to read each other's pages.

Acknowledgement
This exercise comes from the Gurdjieff tradition and specifically from *On Love and Psychological Exercises*, by A.R. Orage, Samuel Weiser Inc, 1998.

From Poem to Story

Level: Advanced

Time: 45 minutes

Preparation: One copy of the poem below for each student.

Dreams
Hold fast to dreams
For if dreams die
Life is a broken-winged bird
That cannot fly.

Hold fast to dreams
For when dreams go
Life is a barren field
Frozen with snow.
(From *The Dream Keeper and Other Poems* by Langston Hughes, New York, 1932.)

Lesson outline

1. Put the word *dreams* on the board, and get every student to write down about 10-15 words that they associate with dreams. Tell them they will be sharing these in groups.

2. Get them into groups of four to share their words.

3. Give out the poem for them to read silently. In fours, they discuss what words from their list match the content of the poem.

4. Individually, they write a story using words and ideas from their discussion. Tell them they will be again sharing these in groups.

5. Let them read out their stories to their group and get the others to comment on them.

Giving a Story Meaning

Level: Post-beginner

Time: Lesson 1: 15–20 minutes
Lesson 2: 40 minutes

Preparation: Lesson 1: none
Lesson 2: get one of your more advanced classes to translate into English the texts written in lesson 1.
You will need to check these translations before giving them back to this class.

Lesson One

1. Discuss with the students what they would like to write about; this very much depends on the age, cultural background and interests of the group. The general topic – be it sports, pets, or what they like to eat – is set for the whole group, but how they deal with it depends on the students themselves.

2. Get them to write up to a page in their mother tongue. Tell them that other students will read what they have written.

3. Collect the texts.

Lesson Two

1. Hand back the mother-tongue texts and English translations.

2. Get the students to copy the English version of their own mother-tongue text. They should choose the layout and writing materials, and illustrate their text as they like. If you have the facilities, they may opt to do the task on the computer.

3. Pair the students and they exchange the texts with their partner. Encourage the writer of the story to help the reader with anything that he or she does not understand.

Acknowledgement

We learnt this technique from Jane Voss in a workshop on Primary English in Hannover.

Habits I No Longer Have

Level: Elementary

Time: 40 minutes

Preparation: Bring to mind some habits you no longer have. To get you thinking, here are some habits that Mario no longer has:
smoking a pipe
cycling into town
dieting
travelling in Europe by train.

Lesson outline

1. Tell the class about five or six habits you no longer have.

2. Ask the students to choose three habits they no longer have and, working individually, to write a paragraph about each. Tell them they will share their texts in groups.

3. Group the students in sixes to read each other's paragraphs.

Variation
Ask the students to work instead on habits that their grandparents have dropped over their long lives.

I Remember

Level: Elementary to intermediate

Time: 20–30 minutes

Preparation: Choose a period of your life you feel good remembering.
Prepare to tell the students a few things:
you remember very clearly
you half–remember
you have an abstract notion of, but without any concrete details.

Lesson outline

1. Put up on the board the three categories above. Tell the students about your clear memories, your half–memories and the things that you can't bring back to mind more than vaguely.

2. Ask them to work on their own, and write 12 sentences about their memories of a good period in their life. Ask them to use one or more of the categories.

3. Ask the students to underline the sentence they like the best of their 12, and tell them this is to be displayed. Each student puts this sentence up on the board and adds their name; have them crowding round the board. (If you have a large class, ask the students to go to the board in batches.)

4. Then ask them to mill about so that they can ask each other for more information about a sentence that interests them.

5. Finally, get the students to correct any glitches in the language on the board.

Acknowledgement
The exercise comes from *Sing me the Creation*, Paul Matthews, Hawthorn Press, 1994.

Letter to Myself Later

Level: Elementary to advanced

Time: 30–40 minutes

Preparation: None.

Lesson outline

1. Warm the group up by asking them to shut their eyes and imagine themselves at some time in the future – it could be this time next year. Ask them to see themselves in their possible future work and home environments. Ask them to notice how they look and what they are wearing.

2. Bring them back into the here-and-now classroom. Pair the students, and ask them to talk to their partner about how they see and hear themselves at this future moment.

3. Ask each student to write a letter to him/herself at this future point. It should start, *Dear Elder Sister/ Brother*. Tell them the letter will be displayed to the class.

4. The partners read each other the letters they have written.

5. Ask the students to put up their letters round the walls, and go and read several other letters.

Note
You will find many more of these sorts of 'time-travel' activities in *Letters* by Burbidge et al., Oxford, 1996.

List Poems

Level:	Elementary to advanced
Time:	10–20 minutes
Preparation:	None.

Lesson outline

1. Dictate the poem below, writing hard words on the board, and explaining or translating them as you go.
   I used to be snow but now I am ice
   I used to be a nose but now I am a sneeze
   I used to be a monkey, but now I am Godzilla
   I used to put my food in my hair, but now I put it in my stomach
   I used to be a teacher but now I am a talking whale
   I used to be a snowman but now I am a puddle.

2. Bring a student to the board as 'secretary' and ask individual students from around the class to dictate the poem back to him or her. Let the students spot any spelling errors that the secretary makes.

3. Tell the students to write their own 12-line *I used to but now* poems. Help them with any words they don't know in English. Tell them they will share their poems in small groups.

4. Group the students in fours to enjoy their poems.

Variation 1
Ask the students to write their own *When I am alone* poems based on this sixth-grader model:
   When I am alone I fight Ninjas
   When I am alone I play with my hamsters
   When I am alone I wrestle with my cushion
   When I am alone I get so bored I draw weird people.

Variation 2

Ask your students to write *Things that drive me crazy* poems. Here is a model:

People who talk too much
People who laugh too much
People who laugh too loud
Parents who worry too much
My friends
Boyfriends
Fear
Acting in the wrong
Acting like some one you are not
Banks
Supermarkets
Mixed vegetables ...

(*Yolanda Spivey, sixth grade*)

Variation 3

Ask your students to write *Sadness seeing* poems, based on this model

Sadness seeing the summer go away
Seeing the birds fly away
Seeing the butterflies die in the spring
Seeing my best friend move away
Seeing people in the street with nothing to eat
Nowhere to go, nothing to do
Seeing Mary choke on her turkey sandwich
Seeing your mother find out when you lie
Seeing your grandmother sick in the hospital.

(group-written by five girls)

Variation 4

Ask your students to write *Quiet* poems:

Restaurants are quiet when people are dating
A motel is very quiet
The dark is always quiet
A snake is silent
An ant is quiet
It is quiet in the park
A lamp is quiet
A window is quiet
It is quiet when you go to your house by yourself
It is quiet when your mother is sleeping
Rabbits are quiet
It is quiet in church
Winter is quiet
Slowly moments are quiet ...

(written by a third-grade native English group)

List Poems

Variation 5

If your students are at an advanced level ask them to write a poem praising a loved person, taking as a model André Breton's poem:

My woman with her forest fire hair
With her heat lightning thoughts
With her hourglass waist,
My woman with her otter waist in the tiger's mouth
My woman with her rosette mouth, a bouquet of enormous stars
With her teeth of white mouse footprints on the white earth
With her tongue of polished amber and glass
My woman with her stabbed Eucharist tongue
With her tongue of a doll that opens and closes its eyes
With her tongue of incredible stone
My woman with her eyelashes in a child's handwriting ...

Acknowledgement

We found the texts above in *The List Poem*, Larry Fagin, Teachers' and Writers' Cooperative, 1991.

Making Lists of Things I Do

Level: Lower to upper intermediate

Time: Lesson 1: 30 minutes
Lesson 2: (*one month later*) 40 minutes

Preparation: None.

Lesson outline

Lesson One

1. Write these headings up on the board:
   Things I like doing now
   Things I am meant to do now
   Things I am likely to start doing soon
   Things I have done recently
   Things I am glad to have stopped doing
   Things they wanted me to do years ago.

2. Ask the students to work on their own, and to write five sentences under each heading. Tell them they will be sharing their text with a partner.

3. Take their writing in, correct it lightly and store it.

Lesson Two

1. Ask them to repeat the same writing exercise. (Some may moan about this ...)

2. Give them back their first text so they can compare the two. Ask each student to read the texts to a couple of classmates.

Acknowledgement

Adapted from *The Therapist´s Toolbox*, Susan Carrel, Sage 2001.

Me in the Picture

Level: Elementary to intermediate

Time: 30–40 minutes

Preparation: None.

1. Give the students a 'picture dictation'. This should be simple and lacking detail, to allow them enough freedom to produce their own interpretation. For example:

    Draw two trees, one on the left and one in the middle of the paper.
    Draw a house next to the right-hand tree in the middle of the paper.
    Draw a person between the two trees.
    Draw a bird in the tree on the left.
    Draw a girl looking out from behind the tree in the middle of the paper.
    Draw some flowers in front of the house.

2. Get the students to draw themselves anywhere in the picture. Tell them the pictures will be displayed.

3. They are then to write a paragraph under the picture, imagining what role they play in the scene.

4. Put the pictures up on the wall for them to look at and read.

Poems Using Names

Level: Intermediate to advanced

Time: 45 minutes

Preparation: None.

Lesson outline

1. Give the students topics that you want them to think about in preparation for a future text or the next chapter in the book, e.g. a*utumn* or *Christmas*.

2. They write their name down at the top of an A4 piece of paper and then exchange it with another person in the class.

3. Using the other learner's name, they write an acrostic poem; suppose the name is *Mario* and the topic is *autumn*:
   Morning mist rising from the meadows,
   Autumn's multi-coloured face,
   Rare sun, storms raging,
   Inky clouds threatening
   Odours of Christmas that lies far ahead.
   Another poem that is based on the name *Christine*, and the topic *Christmas*:
   Christmas is in the mind,
   Hasty cards nearly forgotten
   Roasting chestnuts with memories of times gone by,
   Incense burning in the church,
   Singing carols of long ago,
   Tinselled tree, baubles bright.
   It's just memories
   Never to be.
   Eve of all eve.
   Tell them that their poems will be read by the class.

4. Either put the poems on the wall for everybody to read, or use them to make a class book.

Reacting to a Reading

Level: Intermediate to advanced

Time: 45–50 minutes

Preparation: Prepare to explain to the students a bit about *suttee*, the Hindu custom which has the widow burnt alive on her husband's funeral pyre; and define to yourself your own feelings about the practice.

Lesson outline

1. Explain the Indian practice of suttee to your class. Also tell them your own feelings about the practice.

2. Dictate the following passage to the students. Dictate in a relaxed, upbeat voice.

   Throughout the preparations for her burning alive the widow appears jovial.

   She talks with onlookers. Immediately before her immolation she is handed a mirror. She looks in it and sees her past and future lives, which she narrates to the crowd. She believes in re-incarnation. When the fire is lit, she goes up in flames, without signs of pain. The act seems unforced; no one had bound her to the funeral pyre.

   (Adapted from *Thinking Through Cultures*, p.15, Richard Shweder, Harvard University Press, 1991)

3. Ask each student to write one page in reaction to the above description. Offer a 10–15 minute time limit. Tell them that these will be kept private if they wish.

4. Ask the students to underline the most significant sentence in what they have written.

71 Scenes to Illustrate Feelings

Level: Lower to upper intermediate

Time: 30 minutes

Preparation: Make a copy of the passage below for each student.

We saw people arguing. "Anger," I said.
We saw a woman placing food on an altar. "Respect", I said.
We saw a thief with his head locked in a yoke: "Shame," I said.
We saw a little girl sitting by the river throwing an old net with holes into the shallow part of the water. "Hope," I said.
Later she pointed to a man trying to squeeze a barrel that was too large through a doorway that was too small. "Hope," she said.
But to me that was not hope; that was stupidity, rice instead of brains.

Lesson outline

1. Give out the passage and ask the students to read it.

2. Write these words on the board:
   love   sadness   hate   joy   fear   relief

3. Ask the students to work in pairs and to choose two of the feelings, then write a paragraph, using the model as an example, to describe a scene that illustrates them. Tell them they will be sharing these in groups.

4. Group the students in sixes to read out what they have written.

Note
In an international class you are likely to get very varied values in the interpretation of the words and in the sort of scenes portrayed to illustrate them.

Acknowledgement
The reading is lightly adapted from *The Hundred Secret Senses*, by Amy Tan, Flamingo, 1996.

72

Staircases I have Known

Level: Lower intermediate to advanced

Time: 20-30 minutes

Preparation: Be ready to tell your class about staircases you remember or staircases that are important to you now. This Mario text might set you thinking:

> There was a red spiral staircase that led up to the flat roof of my father's house in Wales. It was outside. As you went up it the view constantly changed: the sea, the mountains, the hillside up from the house ... I wasn´t really allowed up there on my own ... which did not stop me!
>
> In Valdivia, Chile, there was a long, fairly shallow flight of steps that led down from the main street to my large house by the riverbank. There were several kinds of 'landings' or longer steps that took the steepness out of the climb up from the house. We were lucky that our routine meant that we had to carry shopping and stuff down to the house, not up. After the Pinochet coup in Chile an armed soldier often stood on the top step.

But clearly it is **your** staircase memories that will interest your students. **You** are the well of English they draw language water from.

Lesson outline

1. Tell the students about two or three staircases or flights of stairs that you know or have known. If you like drawing, a quick picture might be in order.

2. Ask the students to work in fours and talk about staircases they know or have known.

3. After this oral warm-up ask each student to write about one particularly important set of stairs. Tell the students their texts will be displayed.

4. Have the texts put up round the classroom walls for people to read.

Variations
Other good areas for this kind of writing are:
> Times I have woken up suddenly
> Fire in my experience
> Times I have been a victim
> My history of finding things I've lost.

Rationale
Boredom in language classes can stem from repeating in L2 what one has already thought and said a million times in L1. But the topics offered above are things most students will have never before thought about systematically in the L1. This means that writing about them in English will have a certain freshness and will generate

Things that have Lost their Power

Level: Intermediate to advanced

Time: 30–40 minutes

Preparation: Photocopy the reading:

A large boat that is high and dry in a creek at ebb–tide.
A woman who has taken off her false locks to comb the short hair that remains.
A large tree that has been blown down in a gale and lies on its side with its roots in the air.
The retreating figure of a sumo wrestler who has been defeated in a match.
A man of no importance reprimanding an attendant.
An old man who removes his hat and reveals his thinning hair.
A woman, who is angry with her husband about some trifling matter, leaves home and goes somewhere to hide. She is certain he will rush around looking for her, but he does nothing of the kind. Since she cannot stay away for ever, she swallows her pride and returns.
(From *The Pillow Book of Sei Shonagon*, translated and edited by Ivan Morris, Penguin, 1971.)

Lesson outline

1. Get the students to brainstorm 'things that have lost their power'. Get a student up to the board to jot down what they suggest.

2. Ask each student to write a sentence each about ten things that have lost their power; tell them they will share these in groups.

3. Group the students in sixes to read each other's sentences.

4. Give out the reading.

Ugly Sister-Cinderella Dialogue

Level: Elementary to intermediate

Time: 20–30 minutes

Preparation: None.

Lesson outline

1. Tell the students they are to write a 14-line dialogue between Cinderella and the Ugly Sister. When composing the Ugly Sister's part, they write with their good writing hand, and they do Cinderella's with the other hand. (Students may complain of the difficulty of writing with the wrong hand.) Tell them they will be sharing these dialogues in groups.

2. When they are about half-way through, ask them to swap hands, so they write Cinderella's part with the good hand and her sister's part with the other hand.

3. Group the students in fours or fives to read their dialogues to each other.

Variation
Do the same as above, but without choosing characters for the left and right hands. The dialogue is simply between the two hands.

Rationale
Symbolically, this exercise focuses the student's mind on being either powerful or disempowered. The character expressing themselves through the good writing hand will have a sense of fluency and strength, whereas the opposite is true of the character writing with the other hand.

Acknowledgement
We learnt this technique from Bonnie Tsai, a Pilgrims colleague.

What *Did* Happen?

Level: Lower to upper intermediate

Time: Lesson 1: 10-15 minutes
Lesson 2: 30 minutes

Preparation: Copy the following readings so there is one for each student.

Lesson outline

Lesson One

1. Give out a copy of the texts that follow, and ask the students to read them.

2. Ask for the students' reactions. Have there ever been disagreements about memories in their families? Do the readings ring any bells?

3. As homework, ask the students to talk to their families about times when people have remembered things differently. Their task is write brief reports of events remembered differently by different family members. Tell them that their reports will be displayed to the class.

Lesson Two

1. Group the students in fives, and ask them to read out their homework to each other.

2. Each student sticks their report on the classroom walls – allow a 10-minute reading period, as people go round reading beyond their small group.

3. General discussion.

Three Readings

The grandfather's version (Henry)

I remember it very clearly. Timothy was all excited about his idea of taking a trip to Madrid with us. He was running up to you, Katherine, with a paper on which he had written down what we could do on the trip and when he could go. You waved him away, very tense, saying, "I'm much too upset about this to discuss it with you."

The mother's version (Katherine)

Grandfather and Timothy sat at the table excitedly planning a trip to Madrid, oblivious of the fact that Timothy's brother was sitting nearby, hurt that he was left out of the plans. My father and Timothy came over to me completely focused on their idea, wanting to discuss possible travel dates. I was very irritated that my father, Henry – the adult – was so unaware of how this made Timothy's younger brother feel, and I was also angry that he was encouraging Timothy to get excited about a big trip without first discussing it with me, since I am the mother.

Timothy's version

I wanted to go to Madrid. Grandpa was excited about the idea and we started planning it. When we went over to Mum to discuss travel dates, she said we'd have to discuss it later.

(These readings come from *Context is Everything*, p.19, by Susan Engel, W.H. Freeman, 1999.)

Note

If you are teaching students in an English-speaking environment and if they are staying in host families, the exercise can be done by substituting the memories of the host families for those of the student's own.

SECTION 7
EDITING

Change Your Font

Level: Post-beginner to advanced

Time: Lesson 1: 5 minutes
Lesson 2: 15 minutes

Preparation: None.

Lesson outline

Lesson One

1. Ask the students, for homework, to go to a computer lab or to use their home computer and find a 10-line piece of text they like, on a subject they care about. (A web search will quickly find one.) Ask them to modify the appearance of the text on the computer, playing with typeface, italics, bold, letter size, underlining, etc. to bring out, by using these visual display options, the way they think and feel the text should be read.

2. Explain that this work on fonts will be a prelude to a reading exercise in the next class. Ask them to come to class with a printout of their text, which will be shared in small groups.

Lesson Two

1. Group the students in fours. Ask them each to read their texts to their group.

2. Ask them to then swap texts, and each student then produces a new reading from the way the typography strikes him/her.

3. Allow 5 minutes for general feedback discussion.

Acknowledgement
This exercise is a result of a direct suggestion from John Morgan, (obit Nov 2004) author of *Once Upon a Time*, CUP, 1988.

Choose Your Adjectives

Level: Post beginner to lower intermediate

Time: 15-20 minutes

Preparation: Select a 7-9-sentence story, or a passage of similar length from a unit in your course book that has not yet been done.
The story should have **no adjectives** in it. Delete any that are there. Then photocopy it, one copy per three students.

Lesson outline

1. Give the students some hints about the content of the story, but do not tell them the whole plot.

2. Tell them the story has no adjectives in it and they are going to brainstorm adjectives for it. One person comes to the board to jot down the adjectives the others shout out.

3. Group the students in threes and give out the story. Ask them to incorporate as many of the adjectives on the board as they sensibly can. Tell them they may be sharing their stories with the class.

4. Get several threesomes to read out their stories – some may be hilarious!

Acknowledgement
We learnt this technique from a group of Swedish teachers who came to Pilgrims on a training course in June 1999.

78 Correcting your Students' Writing Mistakes Indirectly

Level: Elementary to advanced

Time: 10-20 minutes

Preparation: Get each of your students an email pen-pal from another class of the same school, or another school in the same country, or another school in a distant place.

Once the correspondences are under way, ask your students to bounce (i.e. Forward to) you an email from their pen-pal that they are happy for other people to read.

From half a dozen of these pen-pals' texts pick out mistakes that your own students often make in their own writing. Copy the texts onto an OHP transparency, or print them onto A3 sheets to display.

Lesson outline

1. Display the texts on OHP or around the room.

2. Spend 15 minutes dramatically and emphatically correcting the mistakes made by the correspondents.

Acknowledgement

We learnt this neat indirect correction technique from a Spanish teacher, Felix Garcia de Salmon, and he used it 15 years ago with hand-written correspondences. Now things are more immediate.

Editing a Poem

Level: Elementary to intermediate

Time: 25–40 minutes

Preparation: Make copies of the text below, one per student.

> A grandmother is a lady who has no children of her own, so she likes other people's boys and girls.
> Grandmas don't have anything to do except to be there. If they take us for walks they slow down past pretty leaves and caterpillars.
> They never say, "Hurry up." Usually they are fat, but not too fat to tie up our shoes.
> They wear glasses and sometimes they can take their teeth out.
> They can answer questions like why dogs hate cats and why God isn't married.
> Grandmas are the only grown-ups who always have time.

Lesson outline

1. Ask the students to shut their eyes, and then read the text to them, slowly. Tell them to put up their hands when they hear bits they don't understand. You may have to re-read it. Note the areas of incomprehension; go over the difficult words, getting the students, where possible, to explain these to each other.

2. Read the passage again, this time as a dictation exercise.

3. Give the students copies of the text so they can correct mistakes they have made.

4. Tell the students that the text was written by an eight-year-old girl thinking about her granny. Ask your students to think about one of their grandmothers, and to change the text so that it becomes true for the person they are thinking about. Also ask them to enrich the text with five more sentences of their own which can go anywhere in the text that they want. Tell them they will be sharing these in groups.

5. Group the students in fours to read and comment on the new texts.

Editing a Poem

Rationale

Some colleagues may question the use of dictation in this activity – why not just give the students copies of the text? In fact, dictation allows the student to slowly absorb the text, to get into it and to think it through. The 'comparing with their own experience' thinking actually gets under way as they are writing, even though you haven't asked them at that point to make the comparison.

Acknowledgement

The text comes from *Sing me the Creation*, Paul Matthews, Hawthorn Press, 1994.

Editing a Short Story

Level: Lower intermediate to advanced

Time: Lesson 1: 3 minutes
Lesson 2: 50 minutes

Preparation: For lesson 1: find a 3–4–page short story that is well within the comprehension ability of your students, and make a copy for each student.
For lesson 2: bring in a few spare sets of scissors, cellophane tape/paper glue, and correction (eg tippex) pen.

Lesson outline

Lesson One

1. Give the students the story, and ask them to read it at home and look up important words they don't know.

2. Ask the students to bring in scissors, tape or glue, and a correction pen for lesson 2.

Lesson Two

1. Explain that they are going to edit the text, chopping out things they don't like, adding in things they feel are needed, changing the order of things in the story etc.

2. Tell them to work on this individually or in pairs; they have 40 minutes for the work. Tell them they can cut and paste the text in any way they want. Tell them they will be sharing these in groups.

3. Bring the students together in small groups and ask them to exchange their texts.

Variation

If you have access to a computer lab, this is much the best place to do this kind of work. For this, you need to have the text in digital form (and you can, of course, forget the scissors etc).

Teacher's quick-reference guide

To use this chart, decide on the lesson-time available to you, and find it in the left-hand column. Then look across the grid till you reach the column showing the standard of your students. (Or start with your students and work down to the time.)

Any filled cell you reach gives you a suitable lesson. And in that same row, the cell in the right-hand column indicates where you'll find it.

NB The first time you run each of these lessons it may take a little longer than shown, especially when you and your students are becoming used to a new way of working.

LESSON TIME (IN MINS)	BEGINNER	POST-BEGINNER	ELEMENTARY	LOWER INT.	INTERMEDIATE	UPPER INT.	ADVANCED	SECTION	LESSON
10-20			Speed writing (Elementary–Advanced)					1	13
10-20			List poems (Elementary–Advanced)					6	66
10-20			Correcting your students' writing mistakes indirectly (Elementary–Advanced)					7	78
15-20		Choose your adjectives (Post-Beginner–Lower Int.)						7	77
15-25		A sentence from a picture (Post-Beginner–Upper Int.)						1	5
20					What I like about cleaning (Intermediate–Advanced)			1	2
20-30				Letters in which students tell you about themselves as writers (Lower Int.–Advanced)				1	1
20-30				Victim-persecutor-rescuer dialogues (Lower Int.–Advanced)				4	44
20-30			I remember (Elementary–Intermediate)					6	64
20-30					Staircases I have known (Intermediate–Advanced)			6	72
20-30			Ugly Sister-Cinderella dialogue (Elementary–Upper Int.)					6	74
20-30					I live (Intermediate)			1	12
20-40			Threesome stories (Elementary–Advanced)					2	29
20-40				Writing to a role (Lower Int.–Advanced)				4	46
20-40			Happy chair, sad chair (Elementary–Advanced)					5	50
25-40			Editing a poem (Elementary–Upper Int.)					7	79
30				Creative start to composition (Lower Int.–Advanced)				1	3
30		A maelstrom of letters (Post-Beginner–Upper Int.)						1	4
30	From word to word (Beginner–Advanced)							1	10
30		I take your day on (Post-Beginner–Upper Int.)						2	23
30		Reality changed from photos (Post-Beginner–Intermediate)						2	26
30				Scenes to illustrate feelings (Lower Int.–Advanced)				6	71
30-40			Chapter headings for my autobiographies (Elementary–Advanced)					1	7
30-40			Things people have written to me (Elementary–Advanced)					1	16
30-40			A younger you (Elementary–Advanced)					2	17
30-40			Hands (Elementary–Upper Int.)					2	22
30-40	Questions to answer and questions not to (Beginner–Advanced)							2	25
30-40			Group stories (Elementary–Advanced)					3	34
30-40		Words to text (Post-Beginner–Advanced)						3	35
30-40		Days of the week write to months of the year (Post-Beginner–Upper Int.)						4	37
30-40		A disguised hand (Post-Beginner–Upper Int.)						4	38
30-40	From group picture to dialogue (Beginner–Elementary)							4	39
30-40					Second-guessing the answer (Intermediate–Advanced)			4	42
30-40			View of a house (Elementary–Advanced)					4	45
30-40			Writing to grammar words (Elementary–Advanced)					4	47

LESSON TIME (IN MINS)	BEGINNER	POST-BEGINNER	ELEMENTARY	LOWER INT.	INTERMEDIATE	UPPER INT.	ADVANCED	SECTION	LESSON
30-40			Written two-way dialogue					4	48
30-40			Your picture, my story					4	49
30-40					Experience that leads to interpersonal writing			5	51
30-40			Different ways of thinking about the same object					6	58
30-40			Letter to myself later					6	65
30-40			Me in the picture					6	68
30-40					Things that have lost their power			6	73
30-40					A trip to remember			1	6
30-40					Dialogue into dialogue			6	57
30-45					Same event-different point of view			4	41
30-45					The whole writes to the parts			4	43
30-45				A composition with no verbs				6	55
30-45					Expanding sentences			2	19
35-40					Ghost-writing			2	21
40		Group holiday fantasy						3	33
40			Habits I no longer have					6	63
40-45					Everyone contributes			3	31
40-50				Sandwich story technique				2	27
40-50					Things said or heard on holiday			2	28
40-50				A flower family				6	56
40-50				Falling				6	59
40-50			From emotion to situation					6	60
45					Concepts			1	8
45					Poems using names			6	69
45						From poem to story		6	61
45-50					Reacting to a reading			6	70
45-60					An extra character			3	30
45-60					Drawing a text			2	18
45-60					News story			3	36

LESSON TIME (IN MINS)	BEGINNER	POST-BEGINNER	ELEMENTARY	LOWER INT.	INTERMEDIATE	UPPER INT.	ADVANCED	SECTION	LESSON
50-60			From my thoughts to our thougts					1	9
50-60				Profiles				2	24
2 & 40-50					Gazing in the mirror			4	40
3 & 50				Editing a short story				7	80
5 & 15			Do I like doing this?					5	52
5 & 15		Change your font						7	76
10-15 & 30				What *did* happen?				6	75
15-20 & 40		Giving a story meaning						6	62
20 & 15				Letters to self				5	54
20-30 & 5-10			Improving on reality					5	53
25 & 30					Expanding questions and answers			3	32
30 & 40				Making lists of things to do				6	67
45 & 45							Essays -1	1	11
45 & 45							Essays -2	1	14
45 & 45-60					Summary writing			1	15
5 & 5 & 15-20				From story to questions to story				2	20